STAR WARS
BOBA FETT™
////////////////// MAN WITH A MISSION

THE REBELLION (from the Battle of Yavin to five years after)
Open resistance begins to spread across the galaxy in protest of the Empire's tyranny. Rebel groups unite, and the Galactic Civil War begins. This era begins with the Rebel victory that secured the Death Star plans, and ends a year after the death of the Emperor high over the forest moon of Endor. This is the era in which the events in *A New Hope*, *The Empire Strikes Back*, and *Return of the Jedi* take place.
The events in these stories take place between one week and ten years after the Battle of Yavin.

STAR WARS
BOBA FETT™

IIIIIIIIIIIIIIIII **MAN WITH A MISSION**

WRITERS
John Wagner • Ron Marz • Thomas Andrews • John Ostrander

ARTISTS
Cam Kennedy • Adriana Melo • Francisco Ruiz Velasco

COLORING
Chris Blythe • Michael Atiyeh

LETTERING
Steve Dutro • Michael David Thomas

COVER ART
Tsuneo Sanda

Dark Horse Books™

publisher
MIKE RICHARDSON

collection designer
M. JOSHUA ELLIOTT

art director
LIA RIBACCHI

series editors
DAVE LAND and RANDY STRADLEY

collection editor
RANDY STRADLEY

assistant editor
DAVE MARSHALL

Special thanks to Leland Chee, Sue Rostoni, and Amy Gary at Lucas Licensing

STAR WARS BOBA FETT: MAN WITH A MISSION

This volume collects issues seven and twenty-eight of the comic-book series Star Wars Empire, as well as the one-shots Star Wars Boba Fett: Overkill *and* Star Wars Boba Fett: Agent of Doom, *all originally published by Dark Horse Comics.*

Published by
Dark Horse Books
A division of Dark Horse Comics, Inc.
10956 SE Main Street
Milwaukie, OR 97222

darkhorse.com
starwars.com

To find a comics shop in your area, call the Comic Shop Locator Service toll-free at 1-888-266-4226

First edition: March 2007
ISBN-10: 1-59307-707-6
ISBN-13: 978-1-59307-707-5

10 9 8 7 6 5 4 3 2
Printed in China

Illustration by Ryan Benjamin, Saleem Crawford, and Chris Blythe

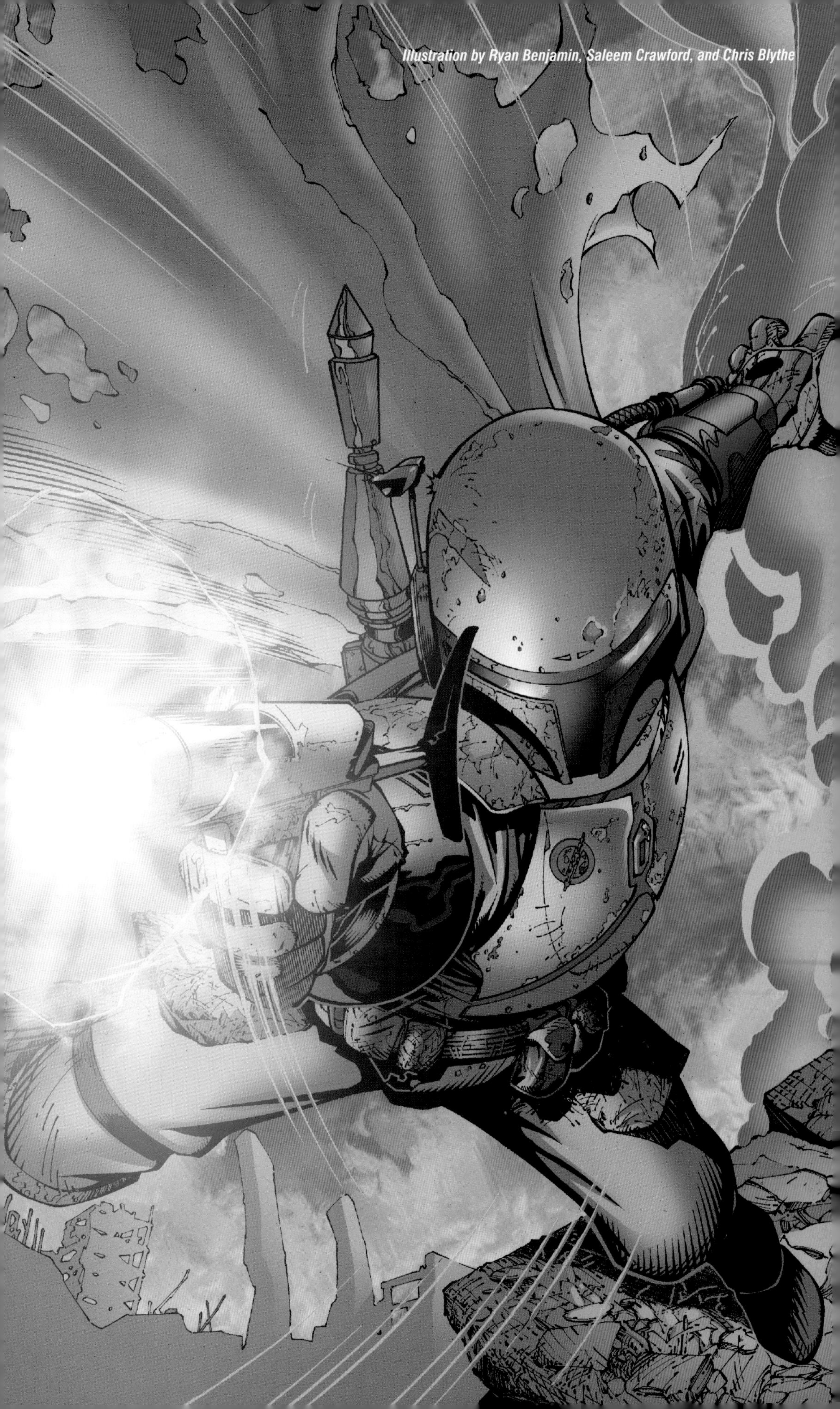

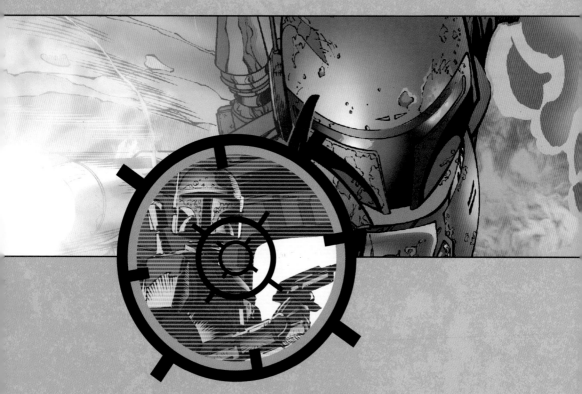

SACRIFICE

SCRIPT
John Wagner

ART
Cam Kennedy

COLORS
Chris Blythe

LETTERS
Steve Dutro

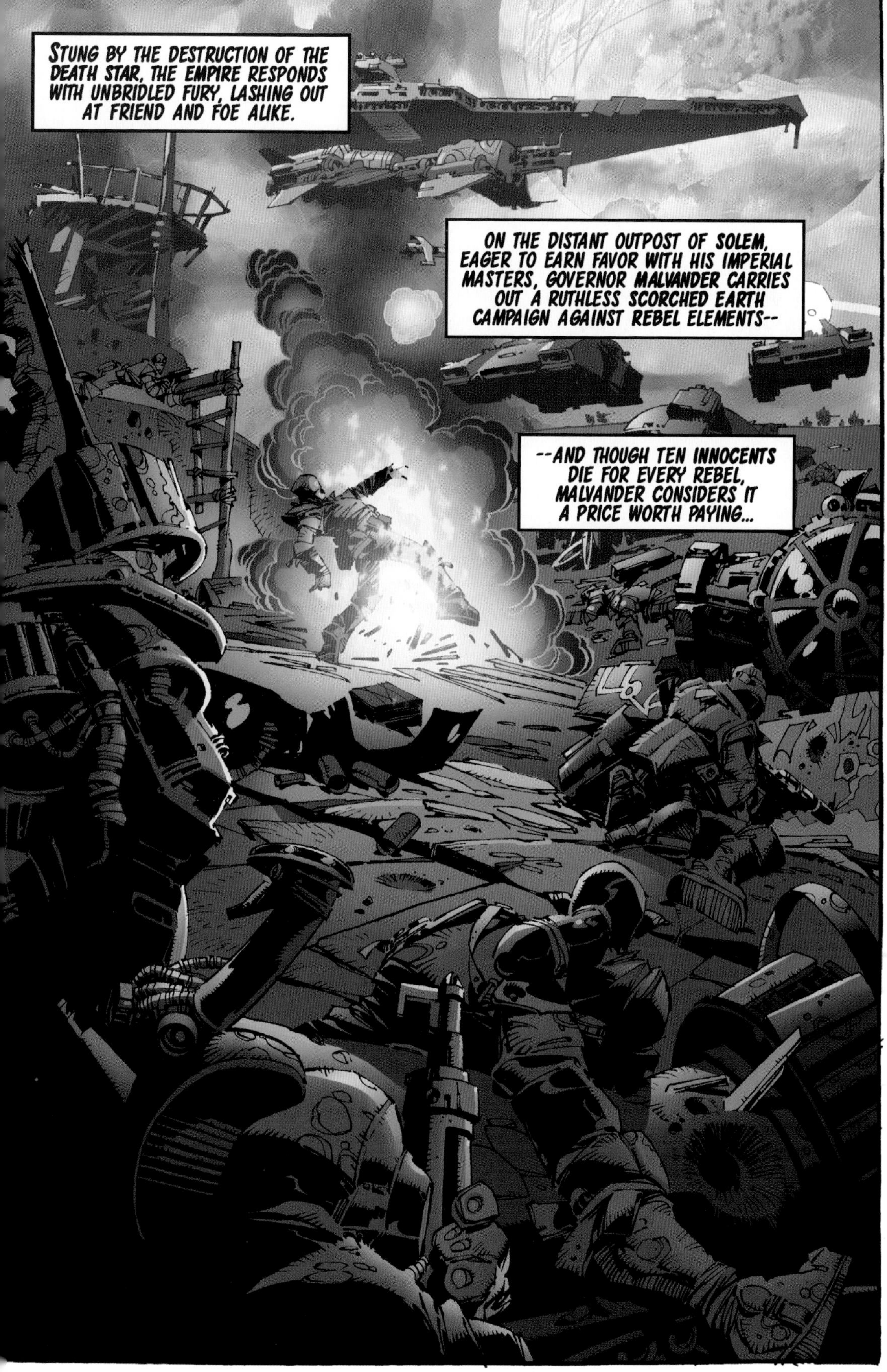
STUNG BY THE DESTRUCTION OF THE DEATH STAR, THE EMPIRE RESPONDS WITH UNBRIDLED FURY, LASHING OUT AT FRIEND AND FOE ALIKE.
ON THE DISTANT OUTPOST OF SOLEM, EAGER TO EARN FAVOR WITH HIS IMPERIAL MASTERS, GOVERNOR MALVANDER CARRIES OUT A RUTHLESS SCORCHED EARTH CAMPAIGN AGAINST REBEL ELEMENTS--
--AND THOUGH TEN INNOCENTS DIE FOR EVERY REBEL, MALVANDER CONSIDERS IT A PRICE WORTH PAYING...

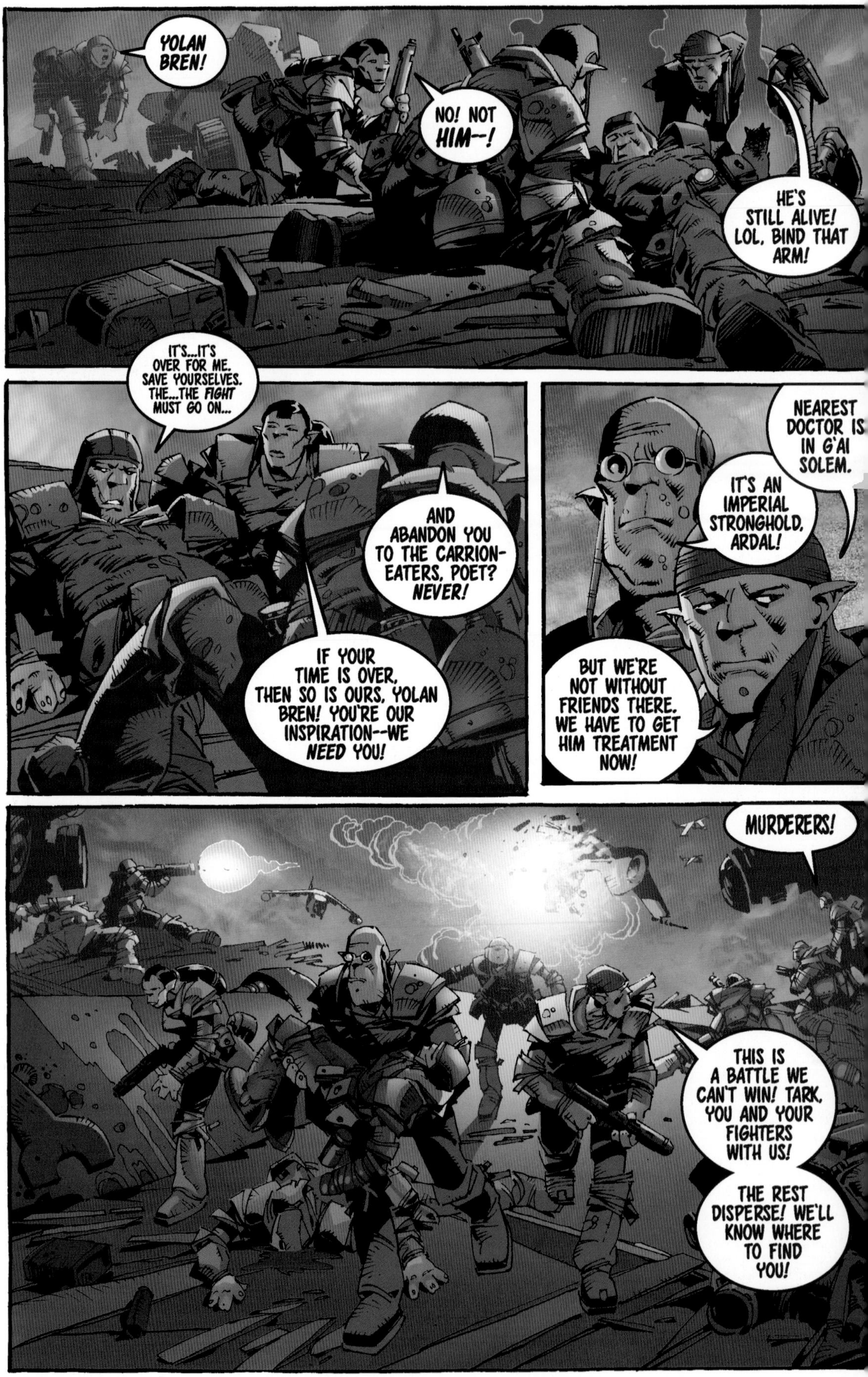
YOLAN BREN!
NO! NOT HIM--!
HE'S STILL ALIVE! LOL, BIND THAT ARM!
IT'S...IT'S OVER FOR ME. SAVE YOURSELVES. THE...THE FIGHT MUST GO ON...
AND ABANDON YOU TO THE CARRION-EATERS, POET? NEVER!
IF YOUR TIME IS OVER, THEN SO IS OURS, YOLAN BREN! YOU'RE OUR INSPIRATION--WE NEED YOU!
NEAREST DOCTOR IS IN G'AI SOLEM.
IT'S AN IMPERIAL STRONGHOLD, ARDAL!
BUT WE'RE NOT WITHOUT FRIENDS THERE. WE HAVE TO GET HIM TREATMENT NOW!
MURDERERS!
THIS IS A BATTLE WE CAN'T WIN! TARK, YOU AND YOUR FIGHTERS WITH US!
THE REST DISPERSE! WE'LL KNOW WHERE TO FIND YOU!

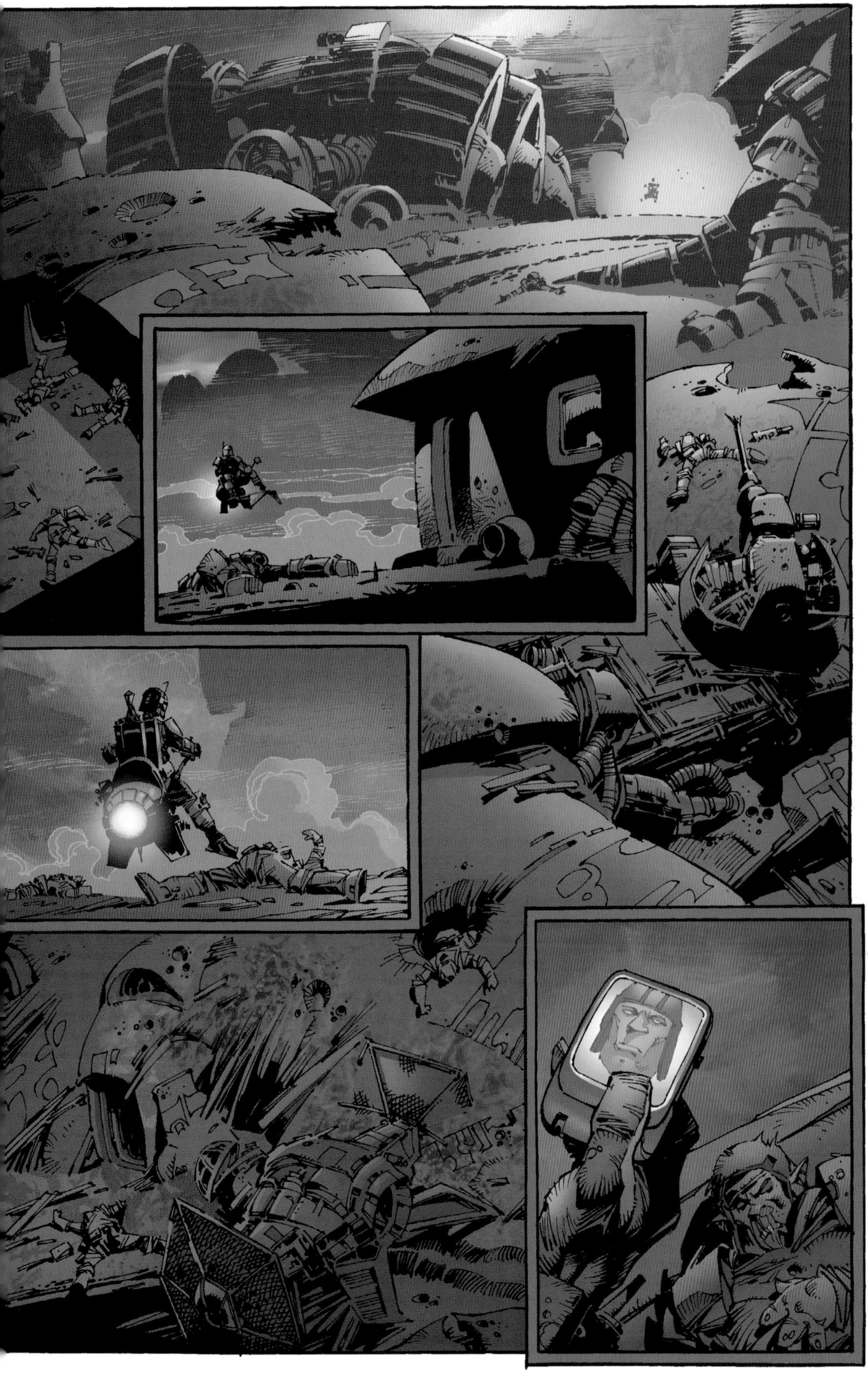

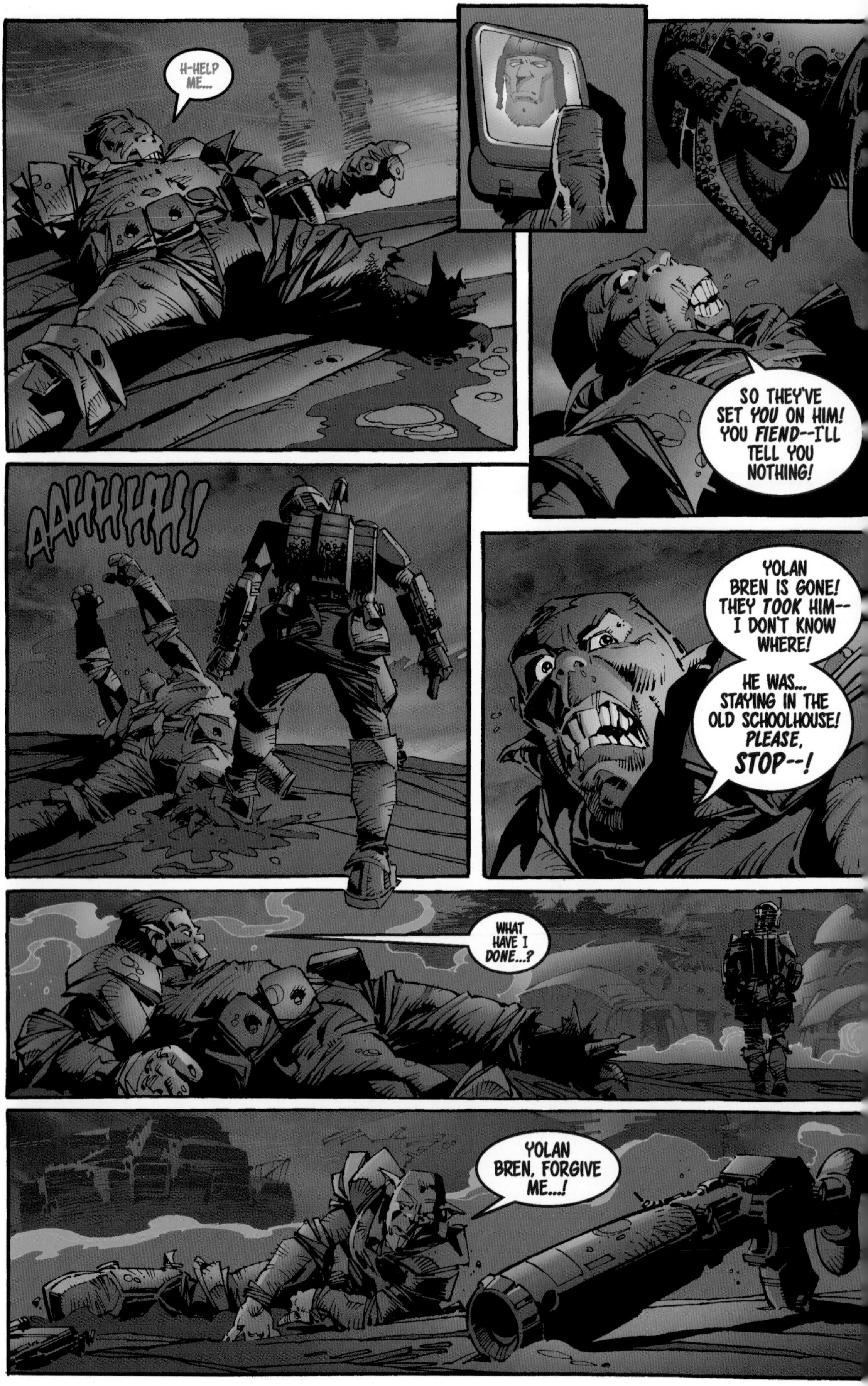
H-HELP ME...
SO THEY'VE SET YOU ON HIM! YOU FIEND--I'LL TELL YOU NOTHING!
AAHHHH!
YOLAN BREN IS GONE! THEY TOOK HIM--I DON'T KNOW WHERE!
HE WAS... STAYING IN THE OLD SCHOOLHOUSE! PLEASE, STOP--!
WHAT HAVE I DONE...?
YOLAN BREN, FORGIVE ME...!

BLIP BLIP

The writing's in code, Fett. I'll compute. Get back to you.

BLEEE

BLOODSUCKER! YOU'LL HAVE HIM OVER MY DEAD--

AAAHHH!

TOOM!

DO IT! YOU'VE KILLED PLENTY OF GOOD MEN BEFORE! WHAT DOES ONE MORE MATTER?

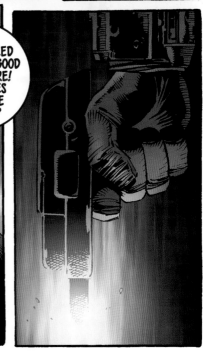

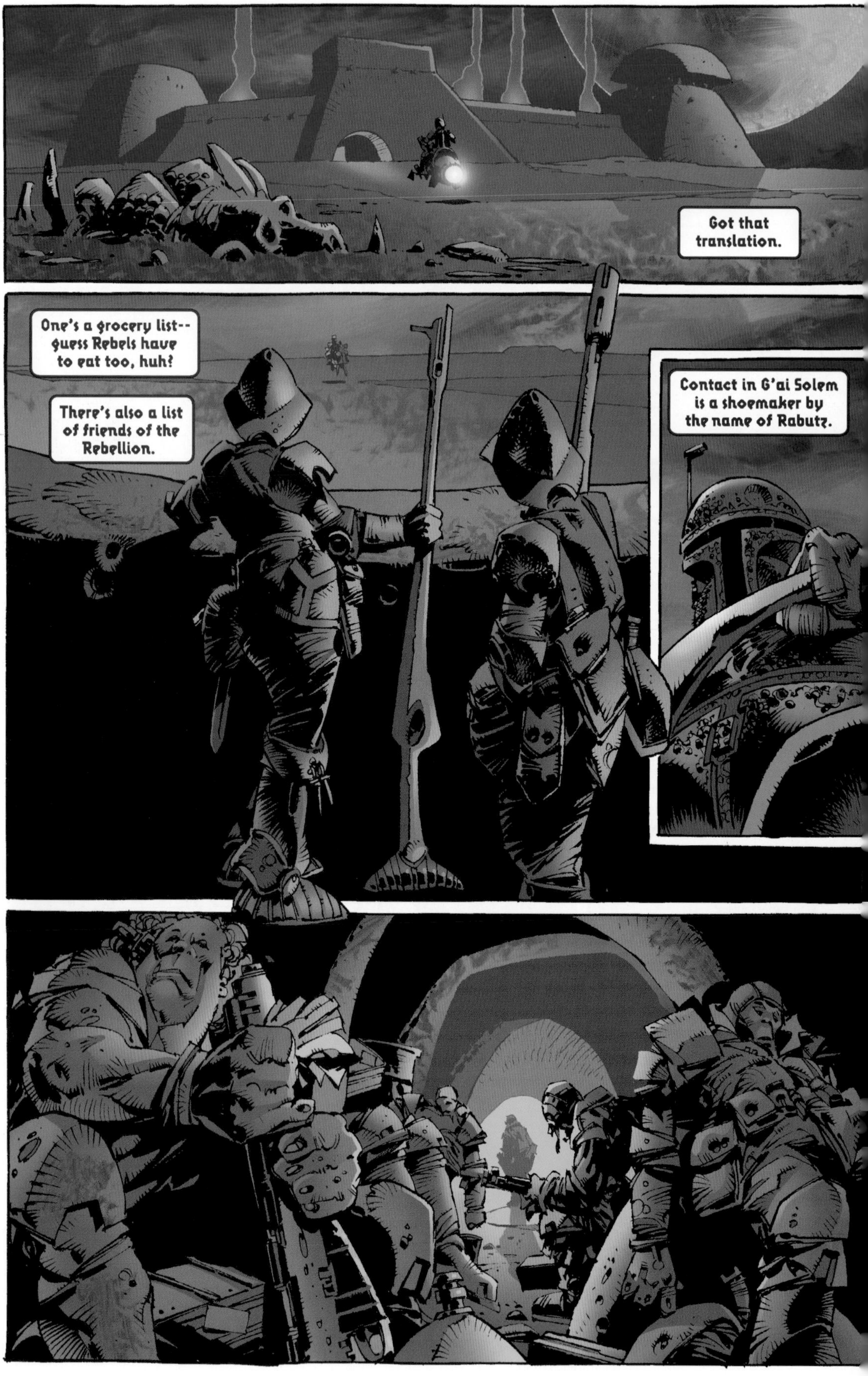
Got that translation.
One's a grocery list--guess Rebels have to eat too, huh?
There's also a list of friends of the Rebellion.
Contact in G'ai Solem is a shoemaker by the name of Rabutz.

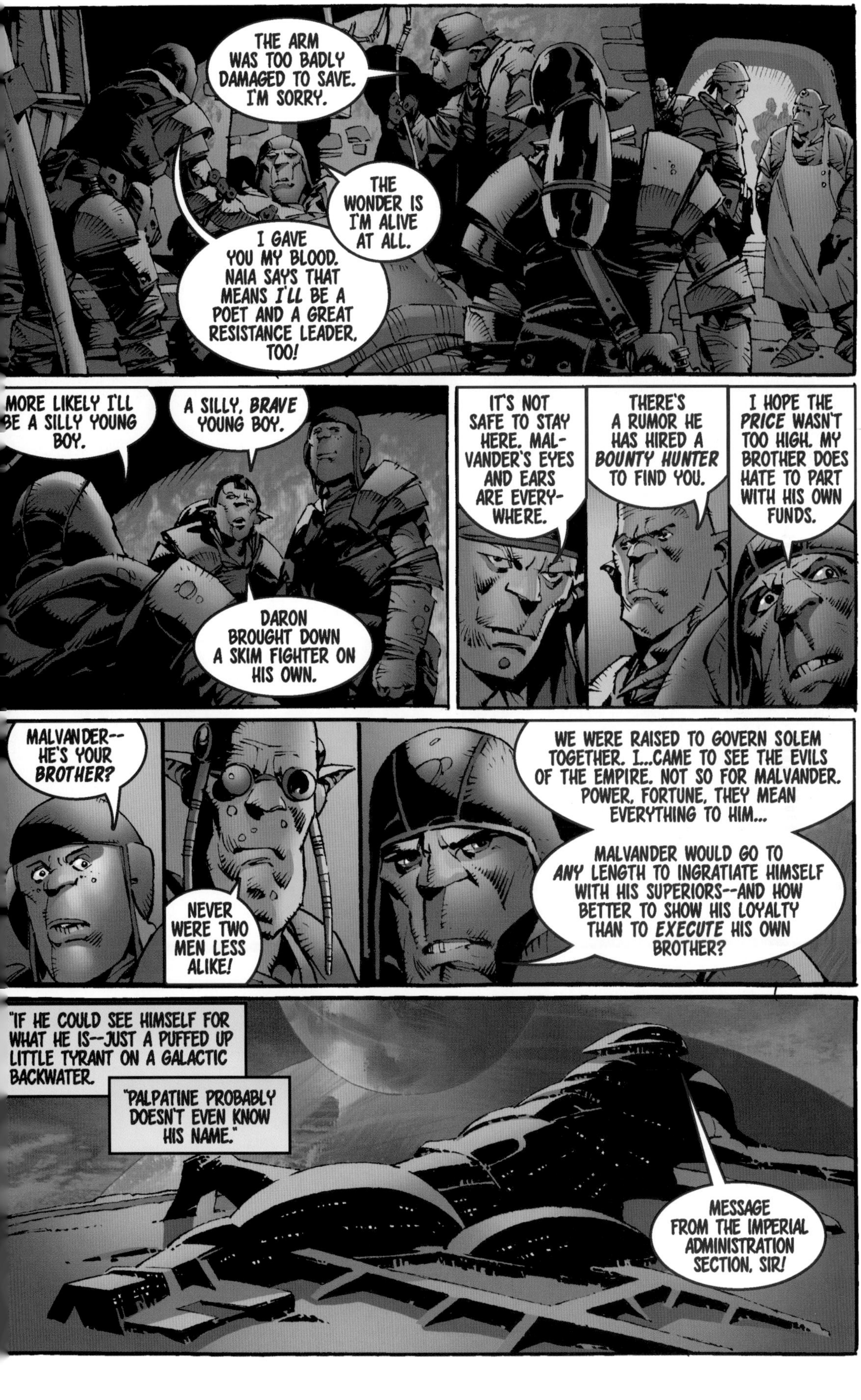

THE ARM WAS TOO BADLY DAMAGED TO SAVE. I'M SORRY.
THE WONDER IS I'M ALIVE AT ALL.
I GAVE YOU MY BLOOD. NAIA SAYS THAT MEANS I'LL BE A POET AND A GREAT RESISTANCE LEADER, TOO!
MORE LIKELY I'LL BE A SILLY YOUNG BOY.
A SILLY, BRAVE YOUNG BOY.
DARON BROUGHT DOWN A SKIM FIGHTER ON HIS OWN.
IT'S NOT SAFE TO STAY HERE. MALVANDER'S EYES AND EARS ARE EVERYWHERE.
THERE'S A RUMOR HE HAS HIRED A BOUNTY HUNTER TO FIND YOU.
I HOPE THE PRICE WASN'T TOO HIGH. MY BROTHER DOES HATE TO PART WITH HIS OWN FUNDS.
MALVANDER--HE'S YOUR BROTHER?
NEVER WERE TWO MEN LESS ALIKE!
WE WERE RAISED TO GOVERN SOLEM TOGETHER. I...CAME TO SEE THE EVILS OF THE EMPIRE. NOT SO FOR MALVANDER. POWER, FORTUNE, THEY MEAN EVERYTHING TO HIM...
MALVANDER WOULD GO TO ANY LENGTH TO INGRATIATE HIMSELF WITH HIS SUPERIORS--AND HOW BETTER TO SHOW HIS LOYALTY THAN TO EXECUTE HIS OWN BROTHER?
"IF HE COULD SEE HIMSELF FOR WHAT HE IS--JUST A PUFFED UP LITTLE TYRANT ON A GALACTIC BACKWATER.
"PALPATINE PROBABLY DOESN'T EVEN KNOW HIS NAME."
MESSAGE FROM THE IMPERIAL ADMINISTRATION SECTION, SIR!

"TO THE GOVERNOR, SOLEM... SIR OR MADAM, ATTENTION--"

SIR OR MADAM? *SIR OR MADAM?*

I-I'M SURE IT'S JUST AN OVERSIGHT, EXCELLENCY.

"IT HAS COME TO OUR NOTICE THAT CURRENT IMPERIAL EXPENDITURE ON SOLEM IS IN SERIOUS *EXCESS* OF BUDGET."

OF *COURSE* IT IS! HOW DO THEY *EXPECT* ME TO ELIMINATE THESE REBEL VERMIN--*STICKS* AND *STONES?*

"AS THE *TAX LEVY* ON SOLEM HAS BEEN *INCREASED* BY 20 PERCENT TO FINANCE IMPERIAL WAR AIMS, WE *REMIND* YOU THAT ANY *SHORTFALL* MUST BE MET FROM YOUR *OWN FUNDS.*"

THEY'RE GOING TO *RUIN* ME! IT'S SO UNFAIR! DON'T THEY UNDERSTAND THERE'S A *LIMIT* TO WHAT I CAN *SQUEEZE* OUT OF THE PEOPLE?

ESPECIALLY AS YOU KEEP KILLING SO MANY OF THEM.

THERE IS ALSO THE MATTER OF BOBA FETT.

THE SECOND PART OF THE *FEE*, SIR--50,000 CREDITS. I'M AT A LOSS TO KNOW WHERE WE'RE GOING TO RAISE IT.

DON'T YOU BOTHER ABOUT FETT! HE'S THE LEAST OF MY WORRIES!

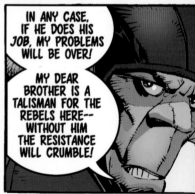

IN ANY CASE, IF HE DOES HIS *JOB*, MY PROBLEMS WILL BE OVER!

MY DEAR BROTHER IS A TALISMAN FOR THE REBELS HERE-- WITHOUT HIM THE RESISTANCE WILL CRUMBLE!

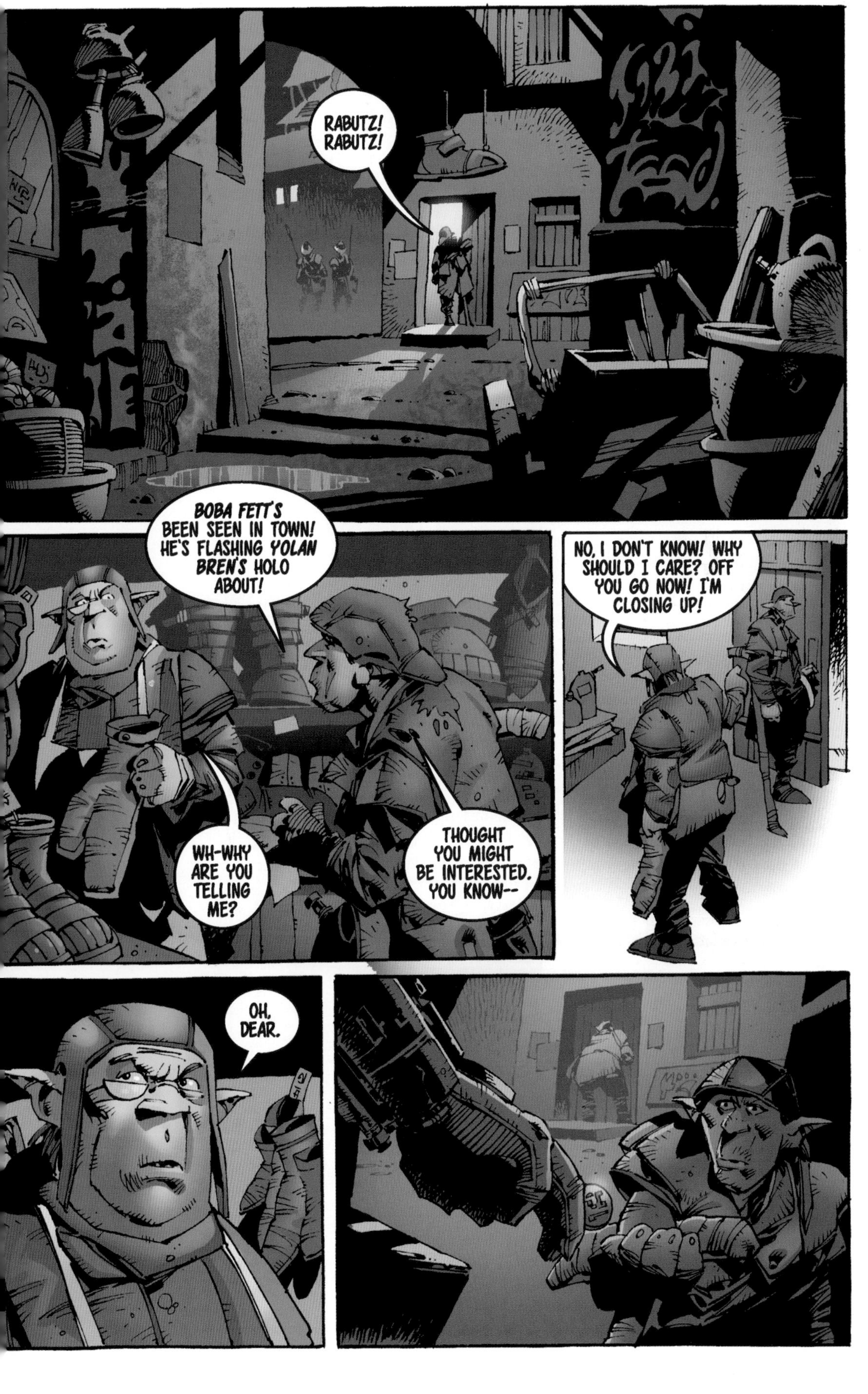
RABUTZ! RABUTZ!
BOBA FETT'S BEEN SEEN IN TOWN! HE'S FLASHING *YOLAN BREN'S* HOLO ABOUT!
WH-WHY ARE YOU TELLING ME?
THOUGHT YOU MIGHT BE INTERESTED. YOU KNOW--
NO, I DON'T KNOW! WHY SHOULD I CARE? OFF YOU GO NOW! I'M CLOSING UP!
OH, DEAR.

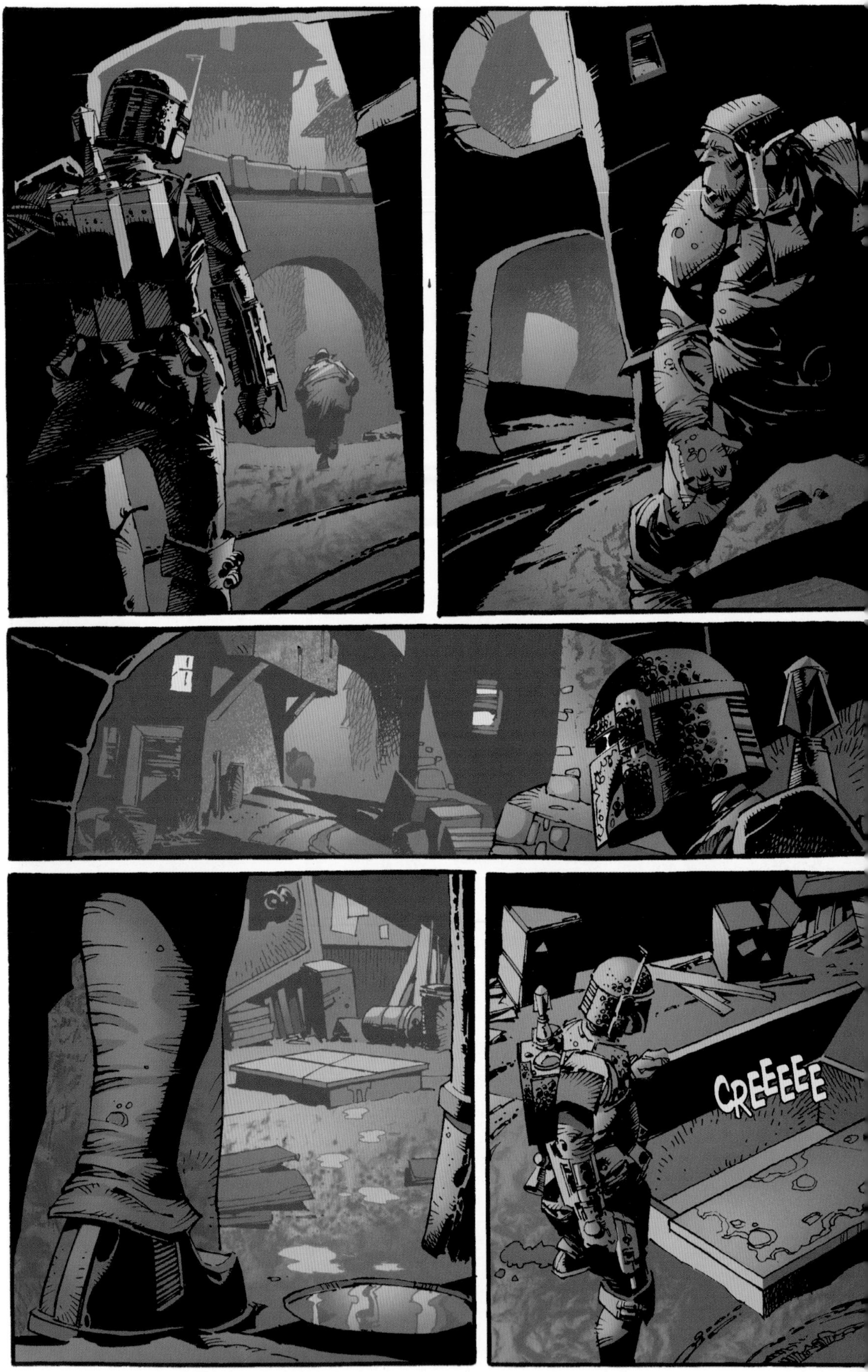
CREEEEE

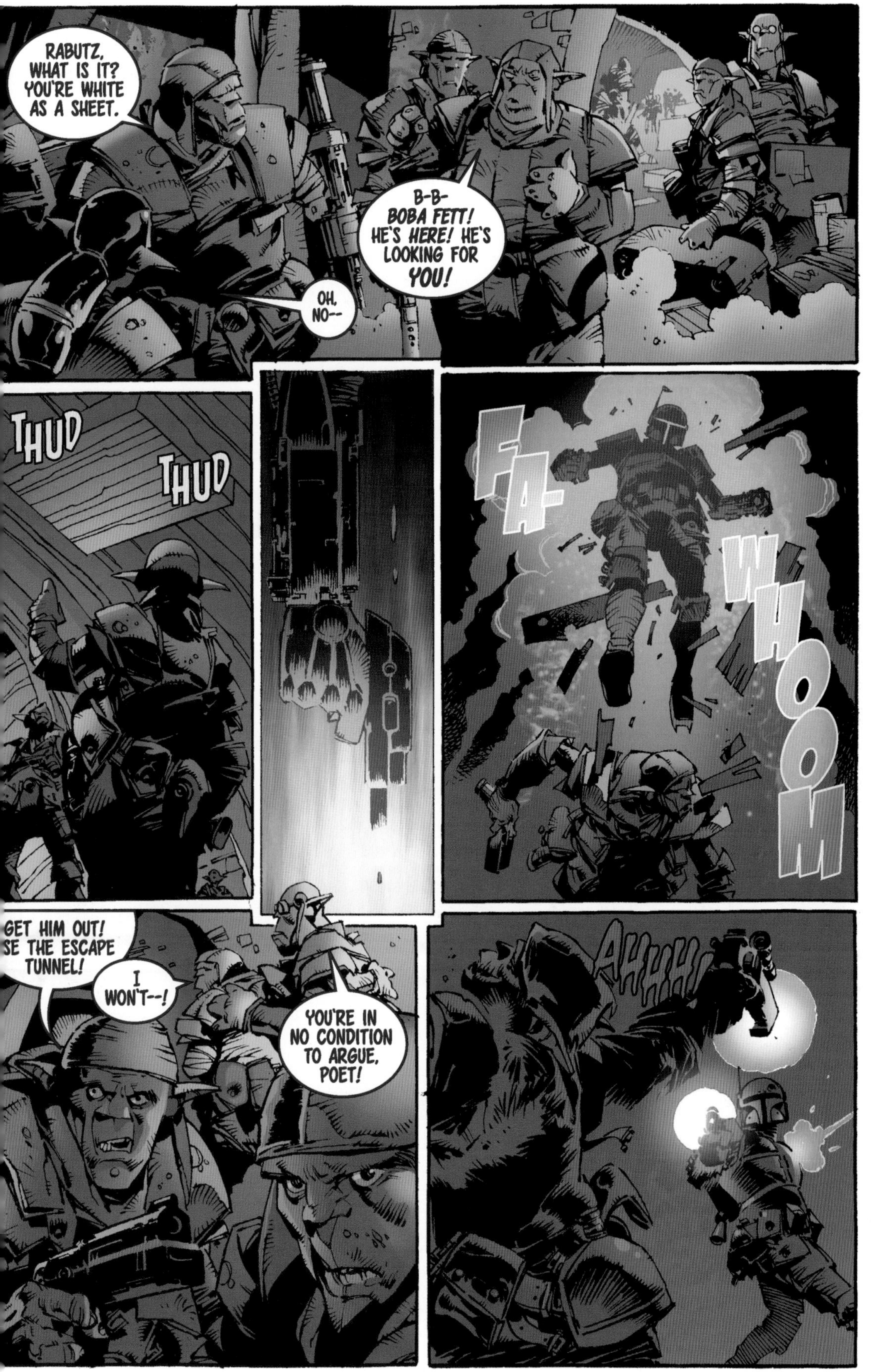
RABUTZ, WHAT IS IT? YOU'RE WHITE AS A SHEET.
B-B- BOBA FETT! HE'S HERE! HE'S LOOKING FOR YOU!
OH, NO--
THUD
THUD
FA-
WHHOOOM
GET HIM OUT! SE THE ESCAPE TUNNEL!
I WON'T--!
YOU'RE IN NO CONDITION TO ARGUE, POET!
AHHH

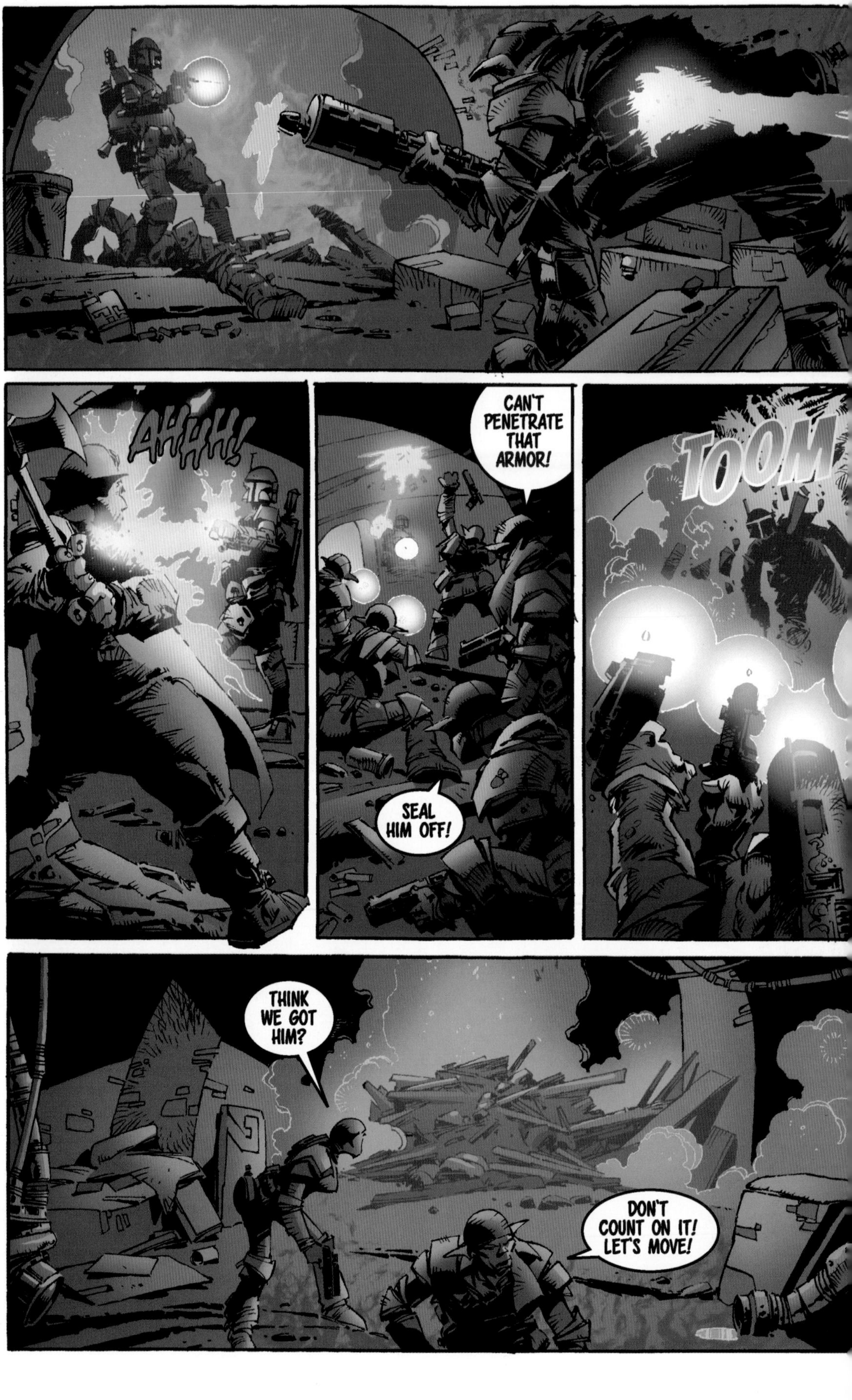
AHHH!
CAN'T PENETRATE THAT ARMOR!
SEAL HIM OFF!
TOOM
THINK WE GOT HIM?
DON'T COUNT ON IT! LET'S MOVE!

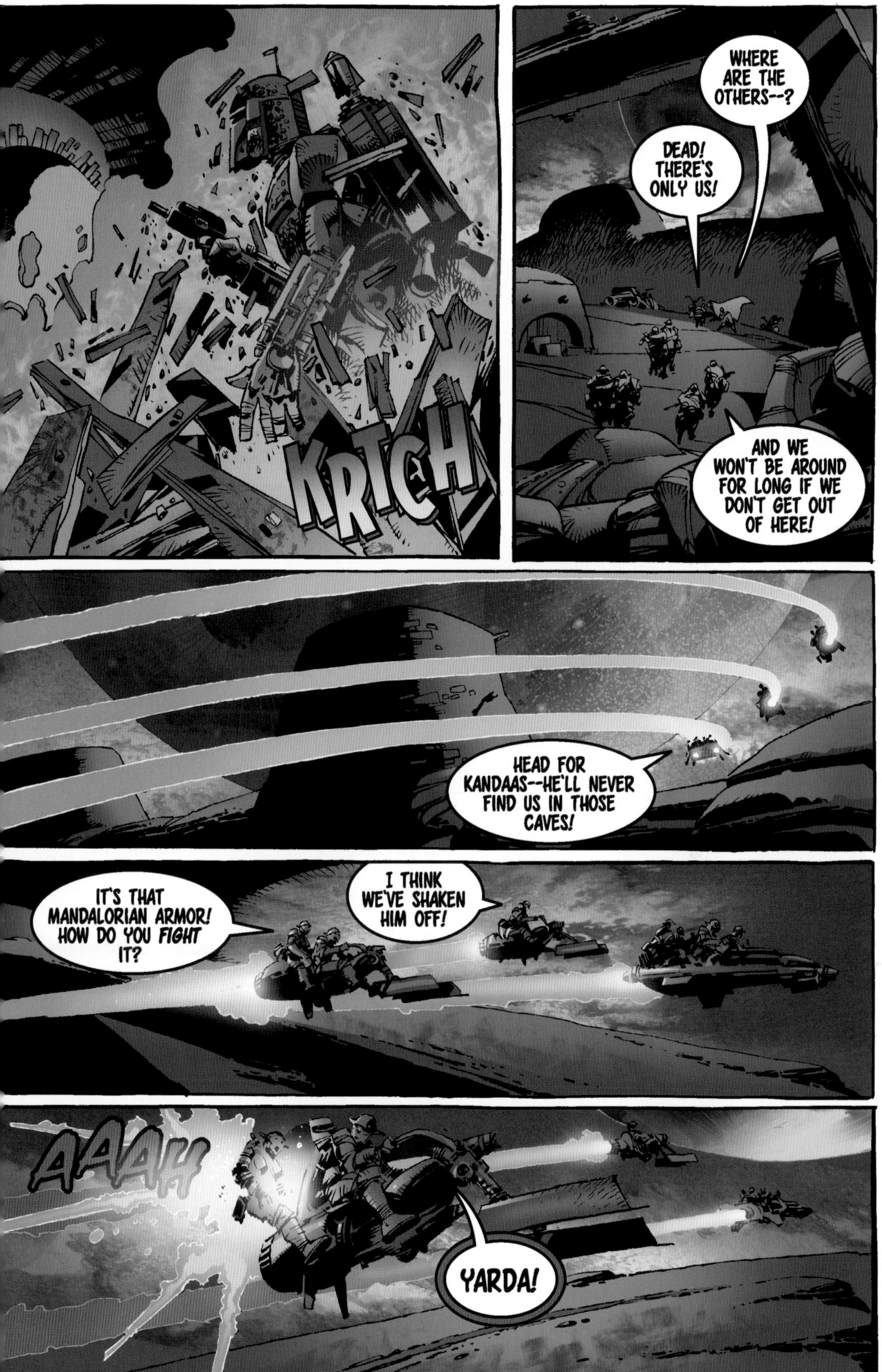
KRTCH
WHERE ARE THE OTHERS--?
DEAD! THERE'S ONLY US!
AND WE WON'T BE AROUND FOR LONG IF WE DON'T GET OUT OF HERE!
HEAD FOR KANDAAS--HE'LL NEVER FIND US IN THOSE CAVES!
IT'S THAT MANDALORIAN ARMOR! HOW DO YOU FIGHT IT?
I THINK WE'VE SHAKEN HIM OFF!
AAAH
YARDA!

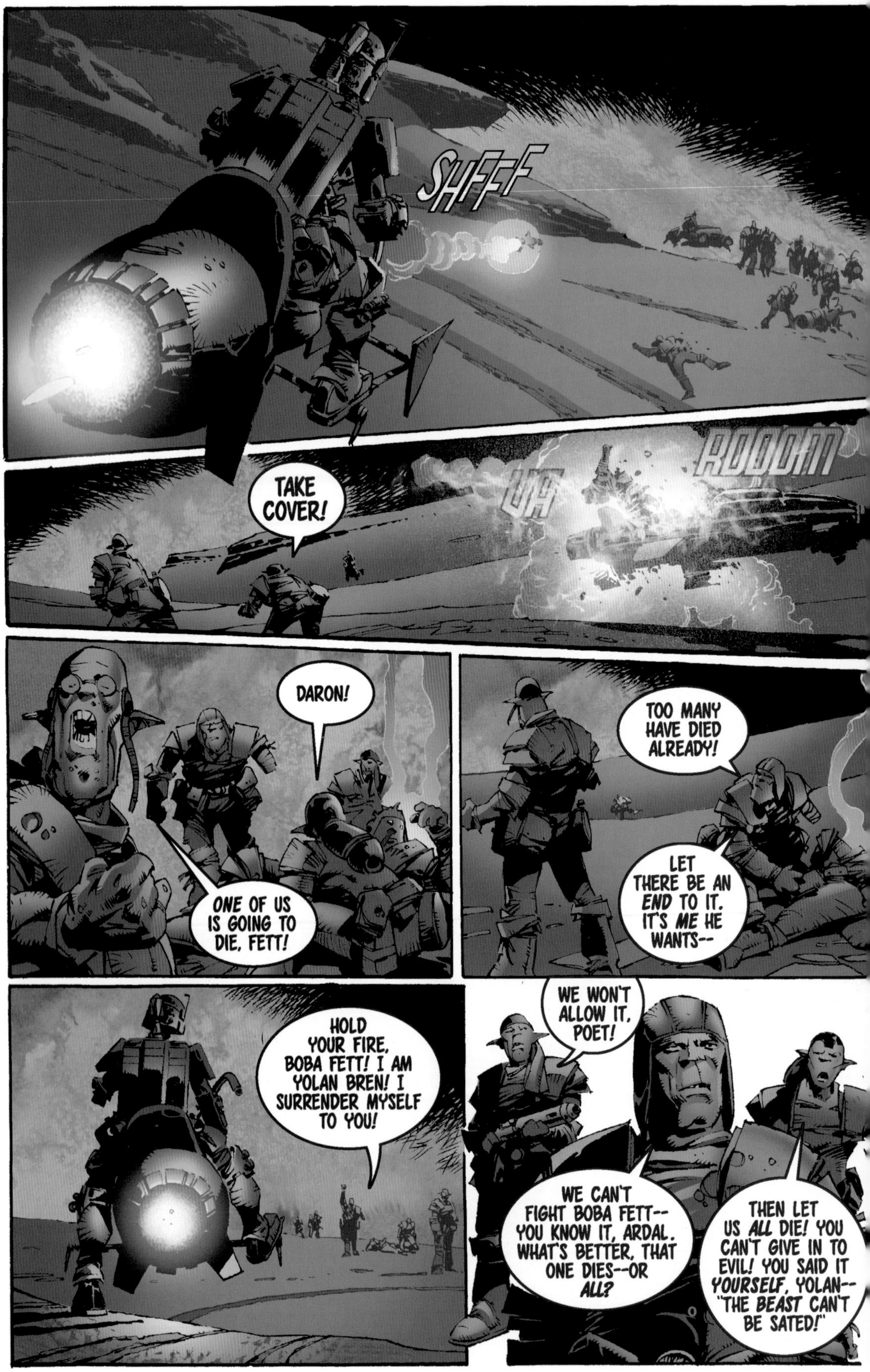

SHFFF
TAKE COVER!
UH
ROOOM
DARON!
ONE OF US IS GOING TO DIE, FETT!
TOO MANY HAVE DIED ALREADY!
LET THERE BE AN END TO IT. IT'S ME HE WANTS--
HOLD YOUR FIRE, BOBA FETT! I AM YOLAN BREN! I SURRENDER MYSELF TO YOU!
WE WON'T ALLOW IT, POET!
WE CAN'T FIGHT BOBA FETT-- YOU KNOW IT, ARDAL. WHAT'S BETTER, THAT ONE DIES--OR ALL?
THEN LET US ALL DIE! YOU CAN'T GIVE IN TO EVIL! YOU SAID IT YOURSELF, YOLAN-- "THE BEAST CAN'T BE SATED!"

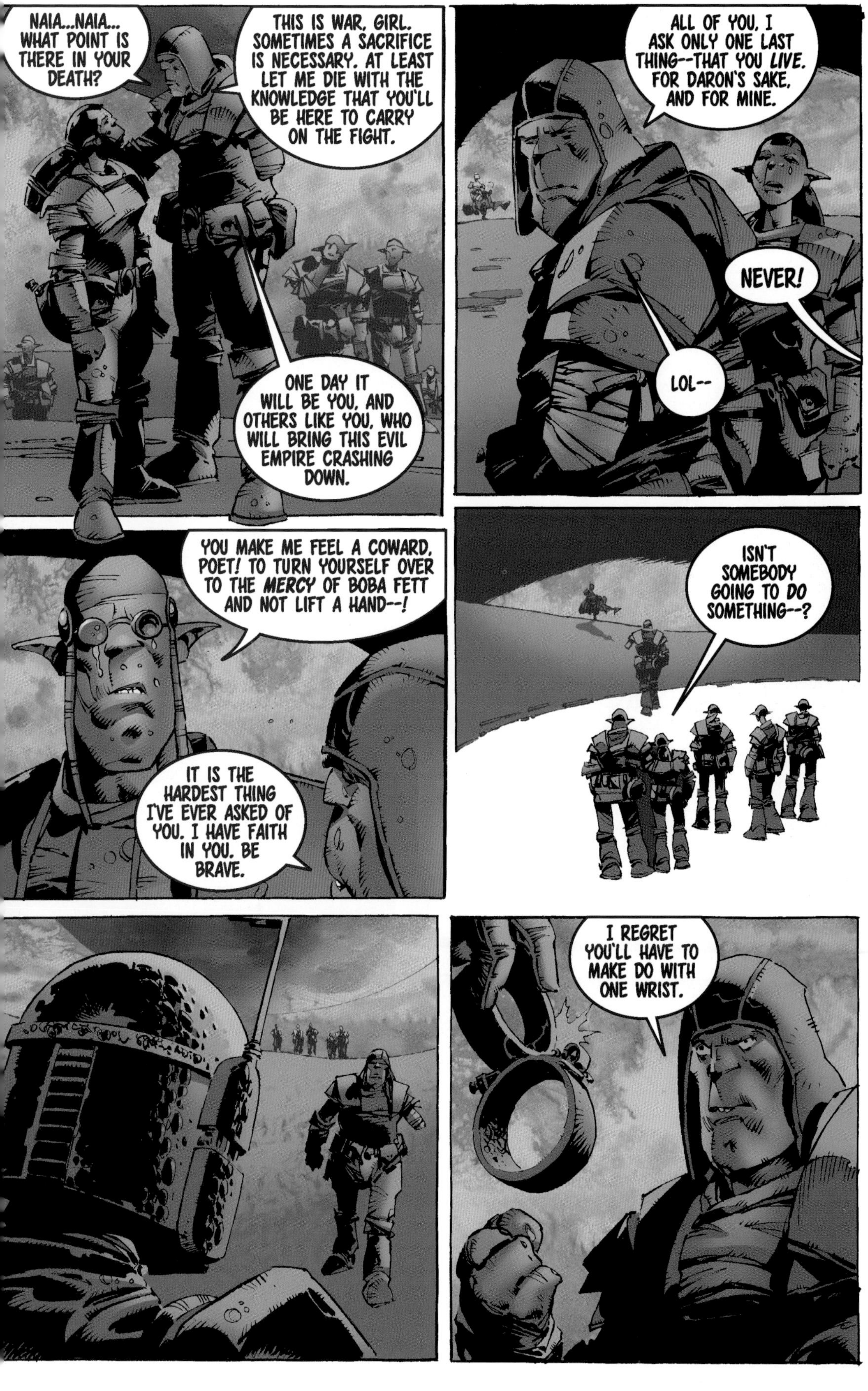
NAIA...NAIA... WHAT POINT IS THERE IN YOUR DEATH?
THIS IS WAR, GIRL. SOMETIMES A SACRIFICE IS NECESSARY. AT LEAST LET ME DIE WITH THE KNOWLEDGE THAT YOU'LL BE HERE TO CARRY ON THE FIGHT.
ONE DAY IT WILL BE YOU, AND OTHERS LIKE YOU, WHO WILL BRING THIS EVIL EMPIRE CRASHING DOWN.
ALL OF YOU, I ASK ONLY ONE LAST THING--THAT YOU LIVE. FOR DARON'S SAKE, AND FOR MINE.
NEVER!
LOL--
YOU MAKE ME FEEL A COWARD, POET! TO TURN YOURSELF OVER TO THE MERCY OF BOBA FETT AND NOT LIFT A HAND--!
IT IS THE HARDEST THING I'VE EVER ASKED OF YOU. I HAVE FAITH IN YOU. BE BRAVE.
ISN'T SOMEBODY GOING TO DO SOMETHING--?
I REGRET YOU'LL HAVE TO MAKE DO WITH ONE WRIST.

FREE YOLAN BREN!
FREE YOLAN BREN!

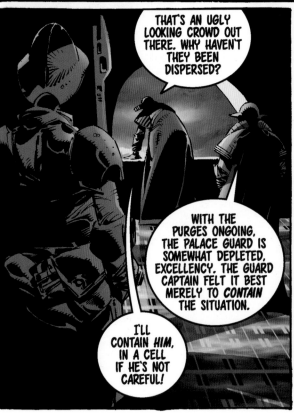

THAT'S AN UGLY LOOKING CROWD OUT THERE. WHY HAVEN'T THEY BEEN DISPERSED?

WITH THE PURGES ONGOING, THE PALACE GUARD IS SOMEWHAT DEPLETED, EXCELLENCY. THE GUARD CAPTAIN FELT IT BEST MERELY TO *CONTAIN* THE SITUATION.

I'LL CONTAIN *HIM*, IN A CELL IF HE'S NOT CAREFUL!

BOBA FETT, SIR!!

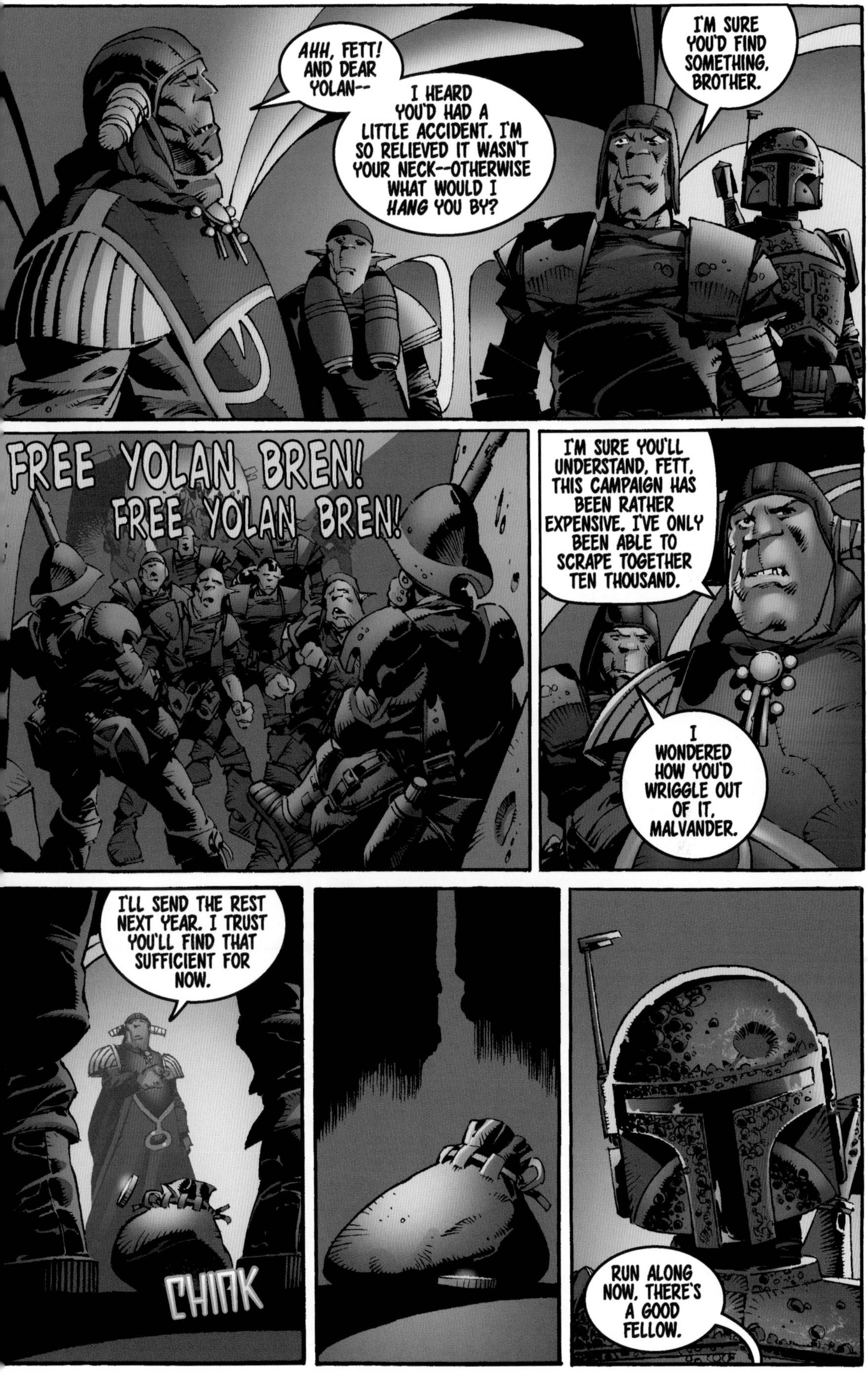
AHH, FETT! AND DEAR YOLAN--
I HEARD YOU'D HAD A LITTLE ACCIDENT. I'M SO RELIEVED IT WASN'T YOUR NECK--OTHERWISE WHAT WOULD I HANG YOU BY?
I'M SURE YOU'D FIND SOMETHING, BROTHER.
FREE YOLAN BREN!
FREE YOLAN BREN!
I'M SURE YOU'LL UNDERSTAND, FETT, THIS CAMPAIGN HAS BEEN RATHER EXPENSIVE. I'VE ONLY BEEN ABLE TO SCRAPE TOGETHER TEN THOUSAND.
I WONDERED HOW YOU'D WRIGGLE OUT OF IT, MALVANDER.
I'LL SEND THE REST NEXT YEAR. I TRUST YOU'LL FIND THAT SUFFICIENT FOR NOW.
CHINK
RUN ALONG NOW, THERE'S A GOOD FELLOW.

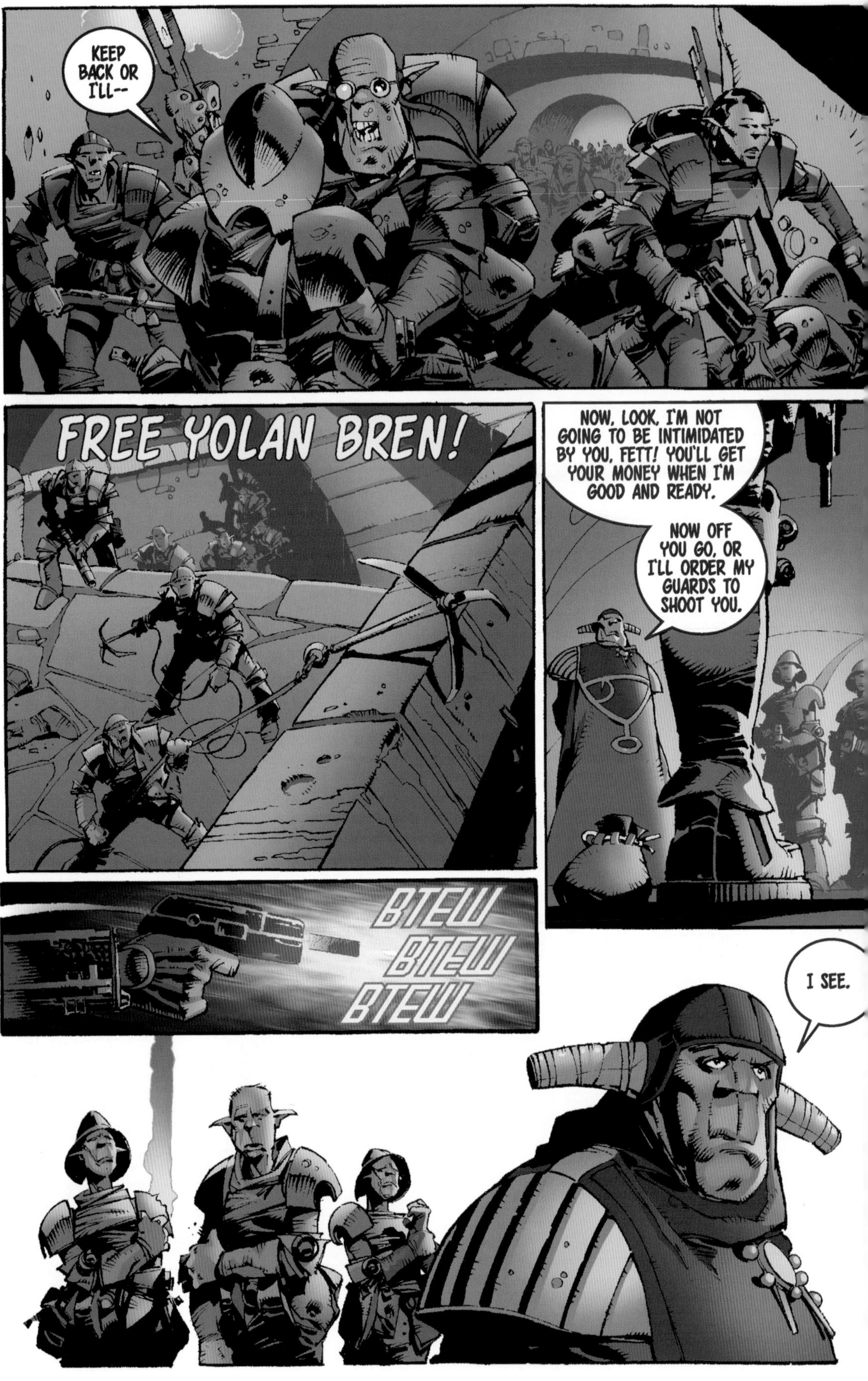
KEEP BACK OR I'LL--
FREE YOLAN BREN!
NOW, LOOK, I'M NOT GOING TO BE INTIMIDATED BY YOU, FETT! YOU'LL GET YOUR MONEY WHEN I'M GOOD AND READY.
NOW OFF YOU GO, OR I'LL ORDER MY GUARDS TO SHOOT YOU.
BTEW BTEW BTEW
I SEE.

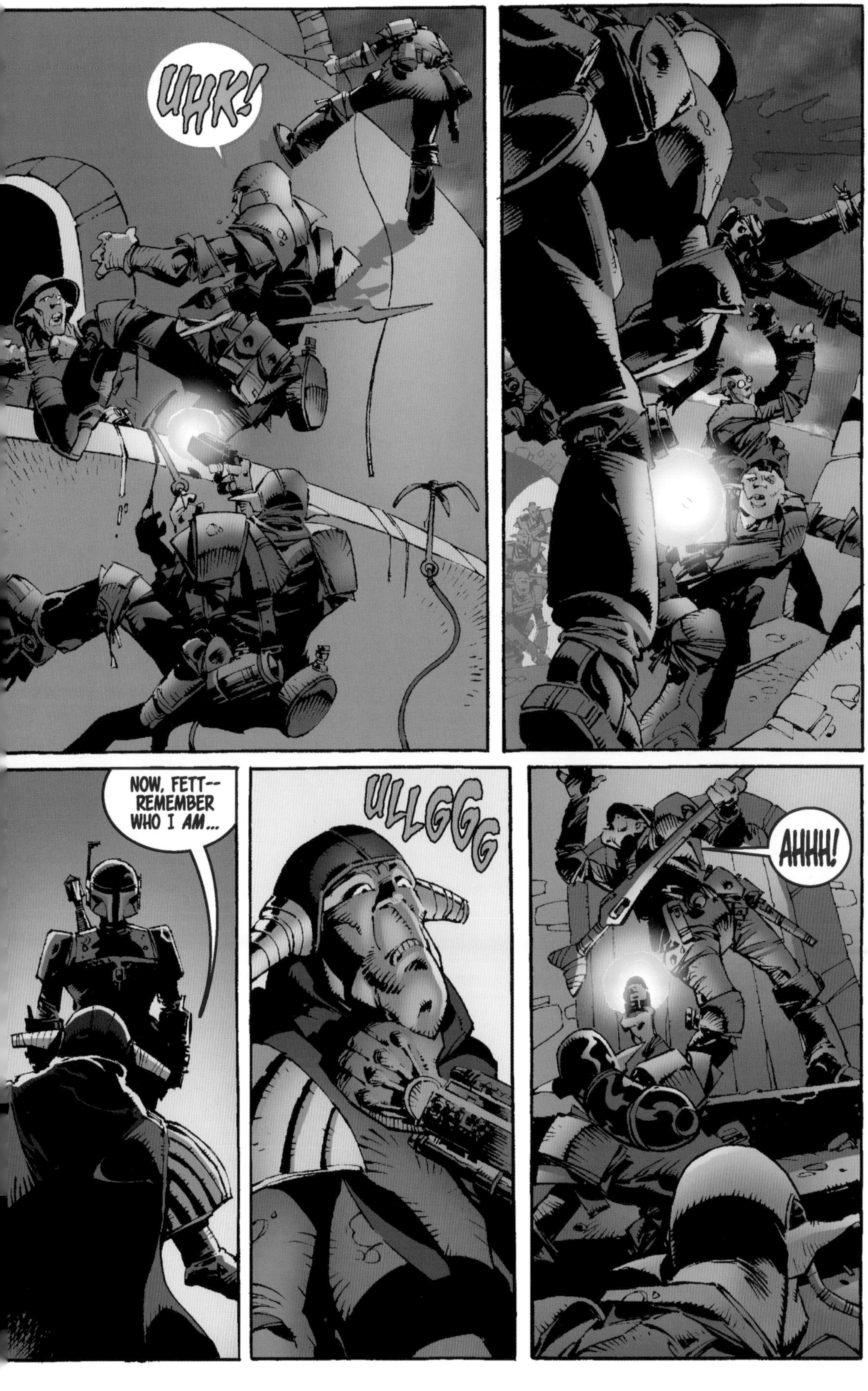
UHK!
NOW, FETT--
REMEMBER
WHO I AM...
ULLGGG
AHHH!

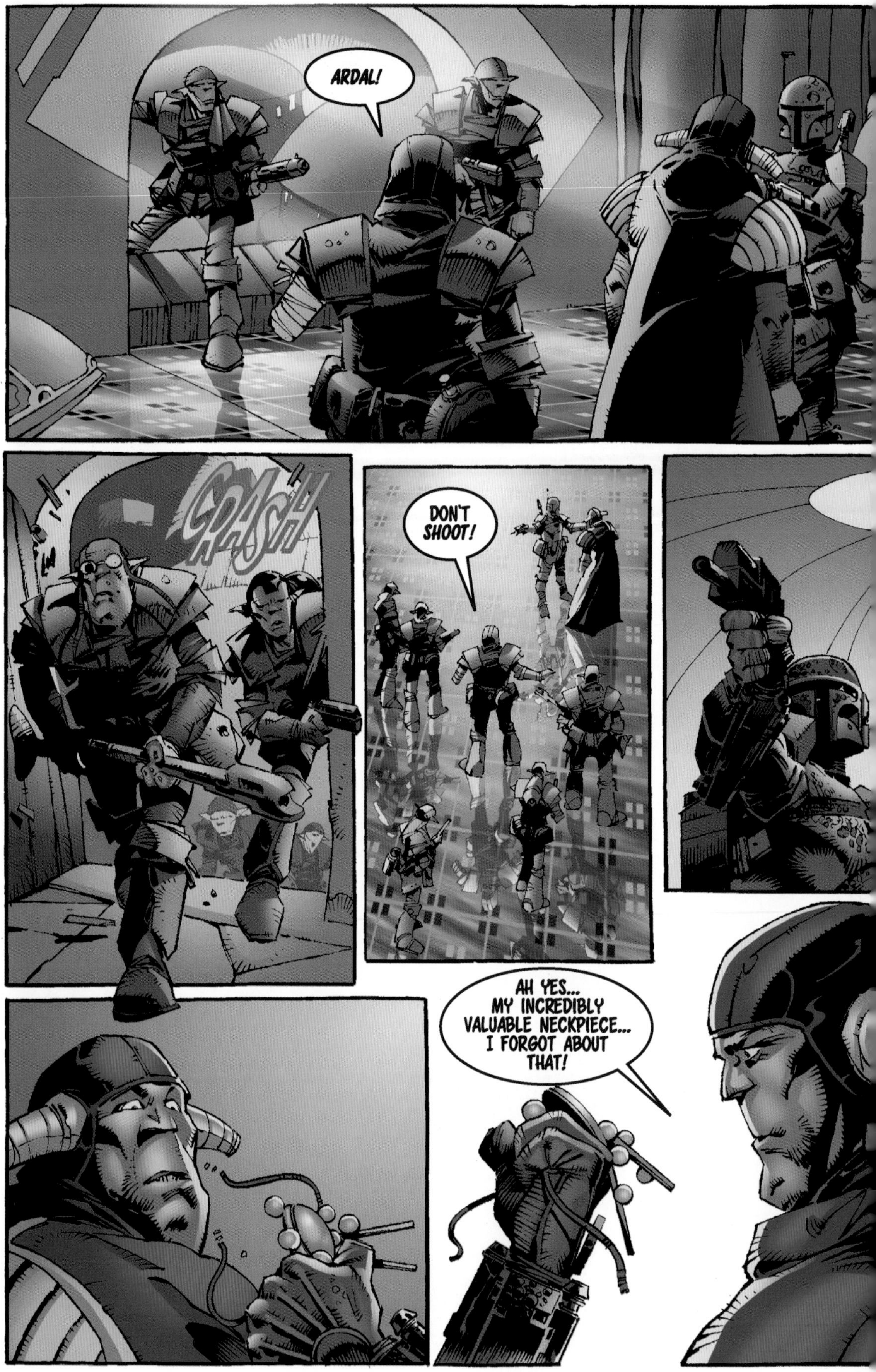
ARDAL!
CRASH
DON'T SHOOT!
AH YES... MY INCREDIBLY VALUABLE NECKPIECE... I FORGOT ABOUT THAT!

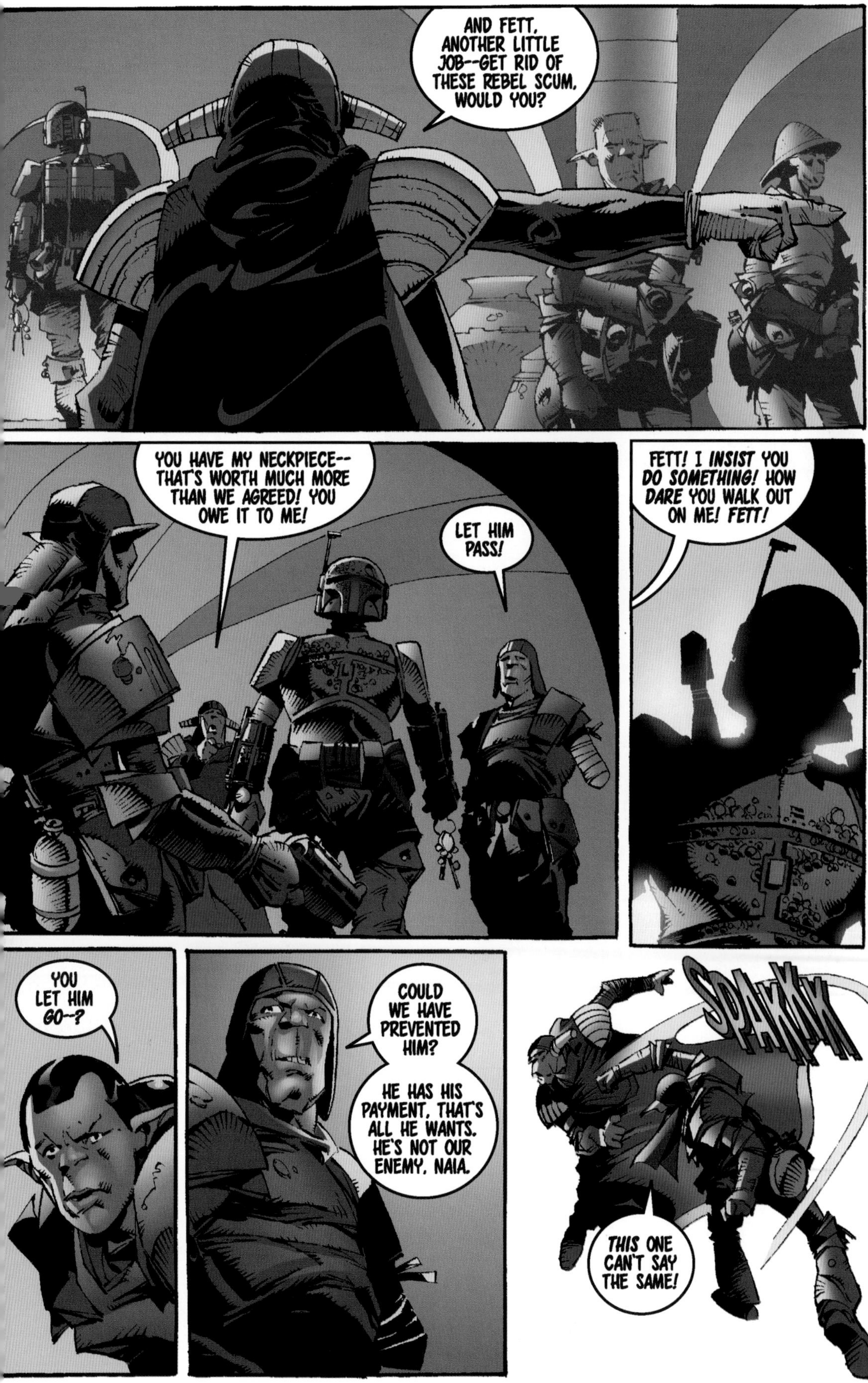
AND FETT, ANOTHER LITTLE JOB--GET RID OF THESE REBEL SCUM, WOULD YOU?
YOU HAVE MY NECKPIECE--THAT'S WORTH MUCH MORE THAN WE AGREED! YOU OWE IT TO ME!
LET HIM PASS!
FETT! I INSIST YOU DO SOMETHING! HOW DARE YOU WALK OUT ON ME! FETT!
YOU LET HIM GO--?
COULD WE HAVE PREVENTED HIM?
HE HAS HIS PAYMENT, THAT'S ALL HE WANTS. HE'S NOT OUR ENEMY, NAIA.
SPAKKK
THIS ONE CAN'T SAY THE SAME!

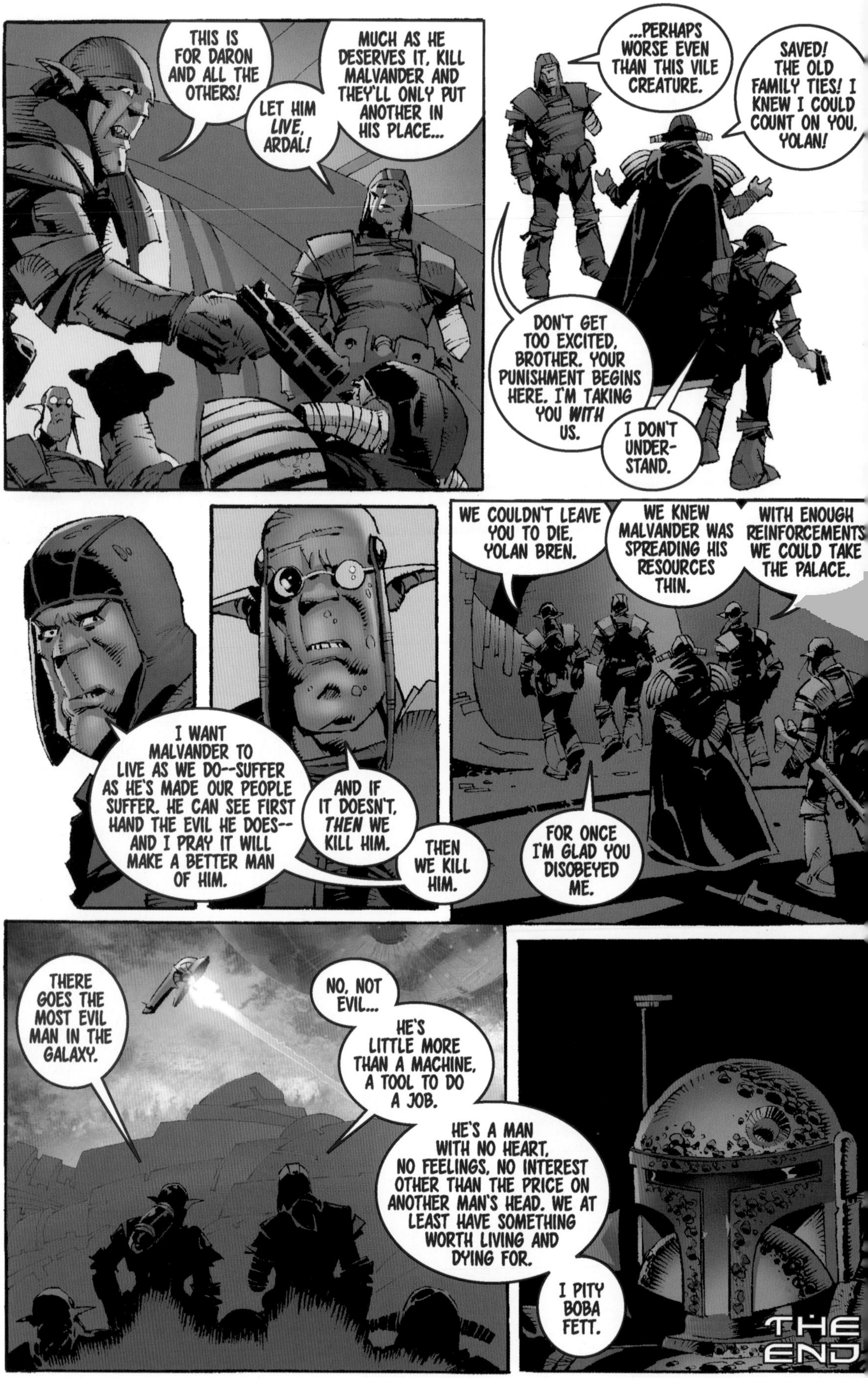
THIS IS FOR DARON AND ALL THE OTHERS!
LET HIM *LIVE*, ARDAL!
MUCH AS HE DESERVES IT, KILL MALVANDER AND THEY'LL ONLY PUT ANOTHER IN HIS PLACE...
...PERHAPS WORSE EVEN THAN THIS VILE CREATURE.
SAVED! THE OLD FAMILY TIES! I KNEW I COULD COUNT ON YOU, YOLAN!
DON'T GET TOO EXCITED, BROTHER. YOUR PUNISHMENT BEGINS HERE. I'M TAKING YOU *WITH* US.
I DON'T UNDER-STAND.
I WANT MALVANDER TO LIVE AS WE DO--SUFFER AS HE'S MADE OUR PEOPLE SUFFER. HE CAN SEE FIRST HAND THE EVIL HE DOES--AND I PRAY IT WILL MAKE A BETTER MAN OF HIM.
AND IF IT DOESN'T, *THEN* WE KILL HIM.
THEN WE KILL HIM.
WE COULDN'T LEAVE YOU TO DIE, YOLAN BREN.
WE KNEW MALVANDER WAS SPREADING HIS RESOURCES THIN.
WITH ENOUGH REINFORCEMENTS WE COULD TAKE THE PALACE.
FOR ONCE I'M GLAD YOU DISOBEYED ME.
THERE GOES THE MOST EVIL MAN IN THE GALAXY.
NO, NOT EVIL...
HE'S LITTLE MORE THAN A MACHINE, A TOOL TO DO A JOB.
HE'S A MAN WITH NO HEART, NO FEELINGS, NO INTEREST OTHER THAN THE PRICE ON ANOTHER MAN'S HEAD. WE AT LEAST HAVE SOMETHING WORTH LIVING AND DYING FOR.
I PITY BOBA FETT.
THE END

Illustration by Tommy Lee Edwards

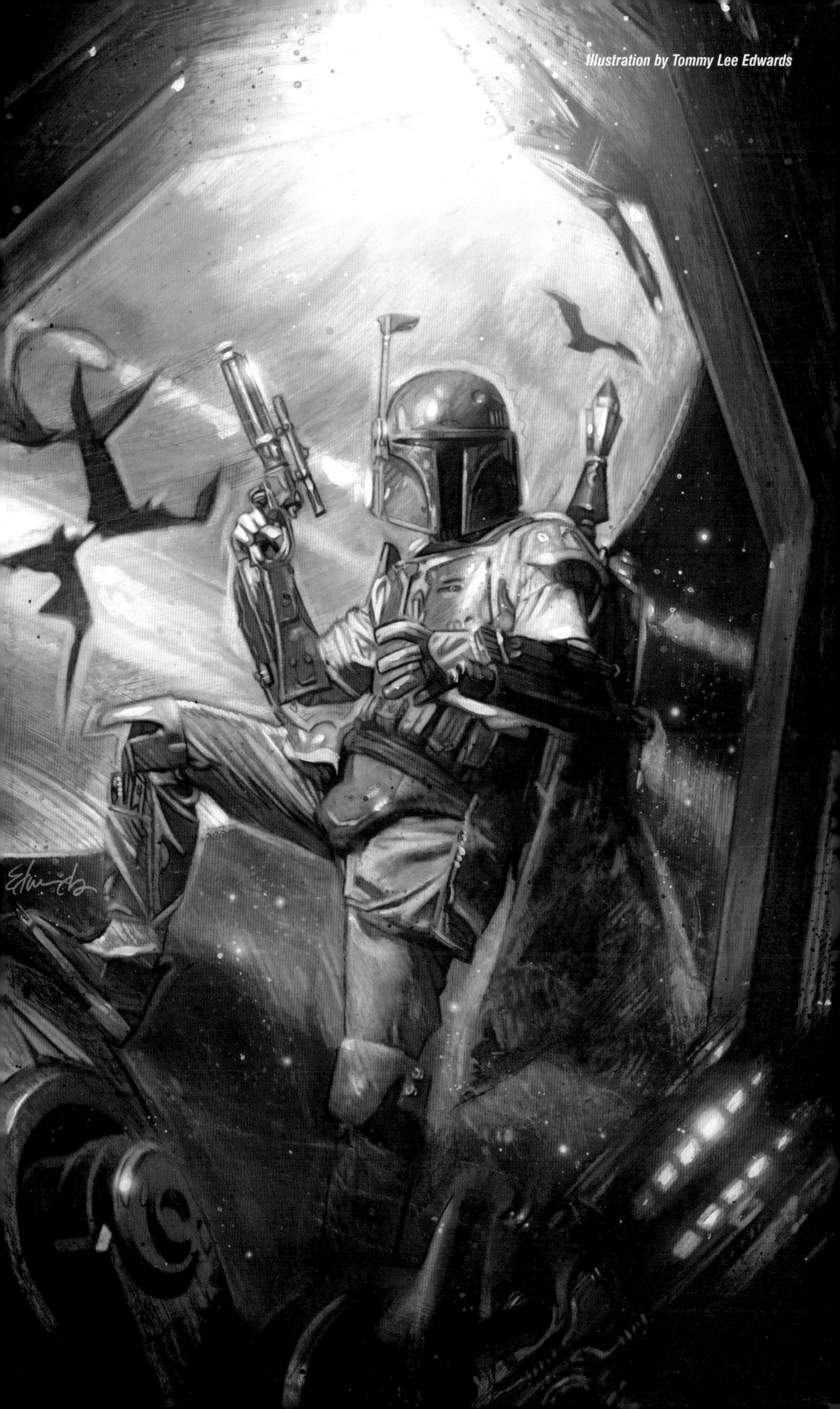

WRECKAGE

SCRIPT
Ron Marz

ART
Adriana Melo

COLORS
Michael Atiyeh

LETTERS
Michael David Thomas

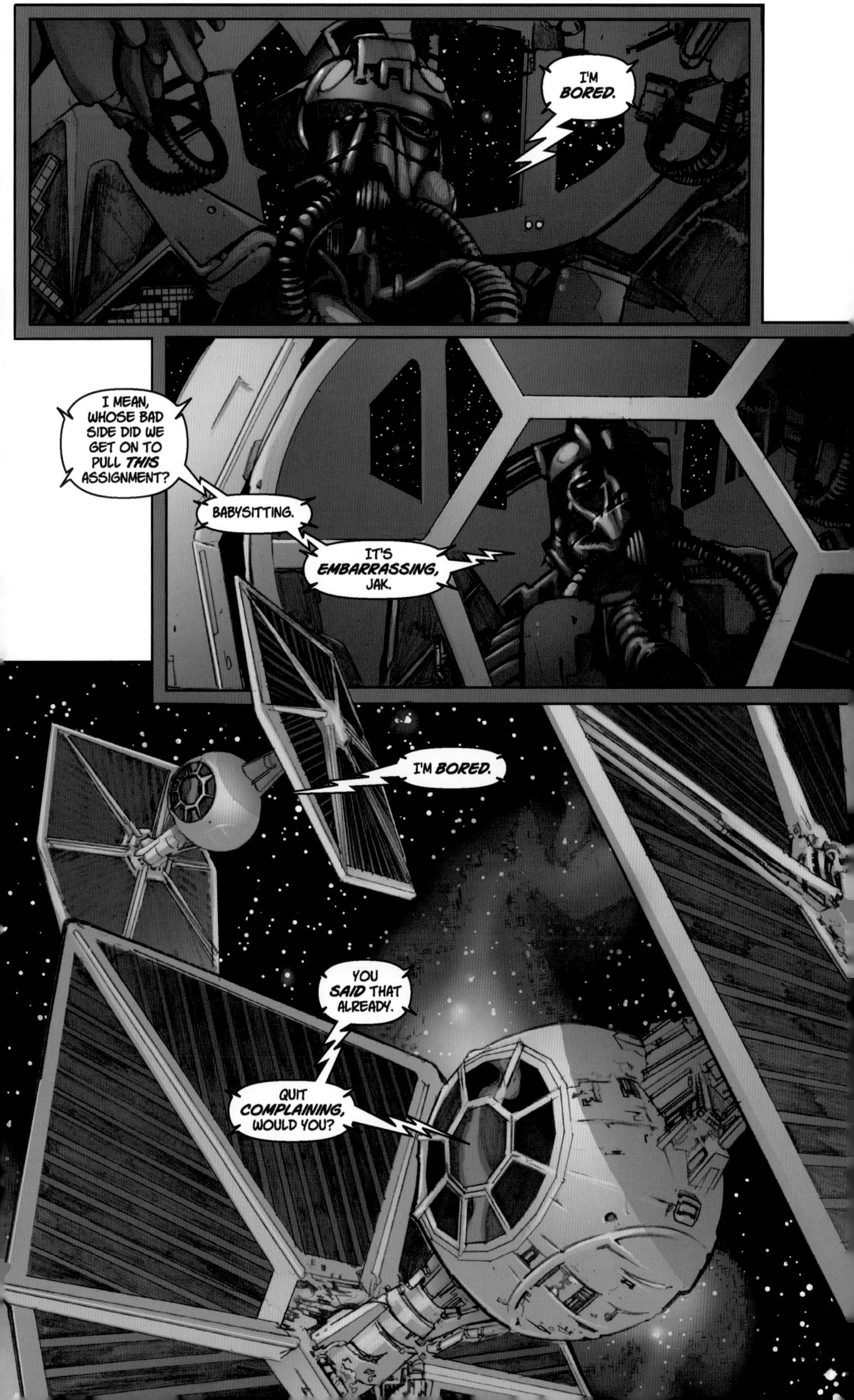
I'M *BORED.*
I MEAN, WHOSE BAD SIDE DID WE GET ON TO PULL *THIS* ASSIGNMENT?
BABYSITTING.
IT'S *EMBARRASSING,* JAK.
I'M *BORED.*
YOU *SAID* THAT ALREADY.
QUIT *COMPLAINING,* WOULD YOU?

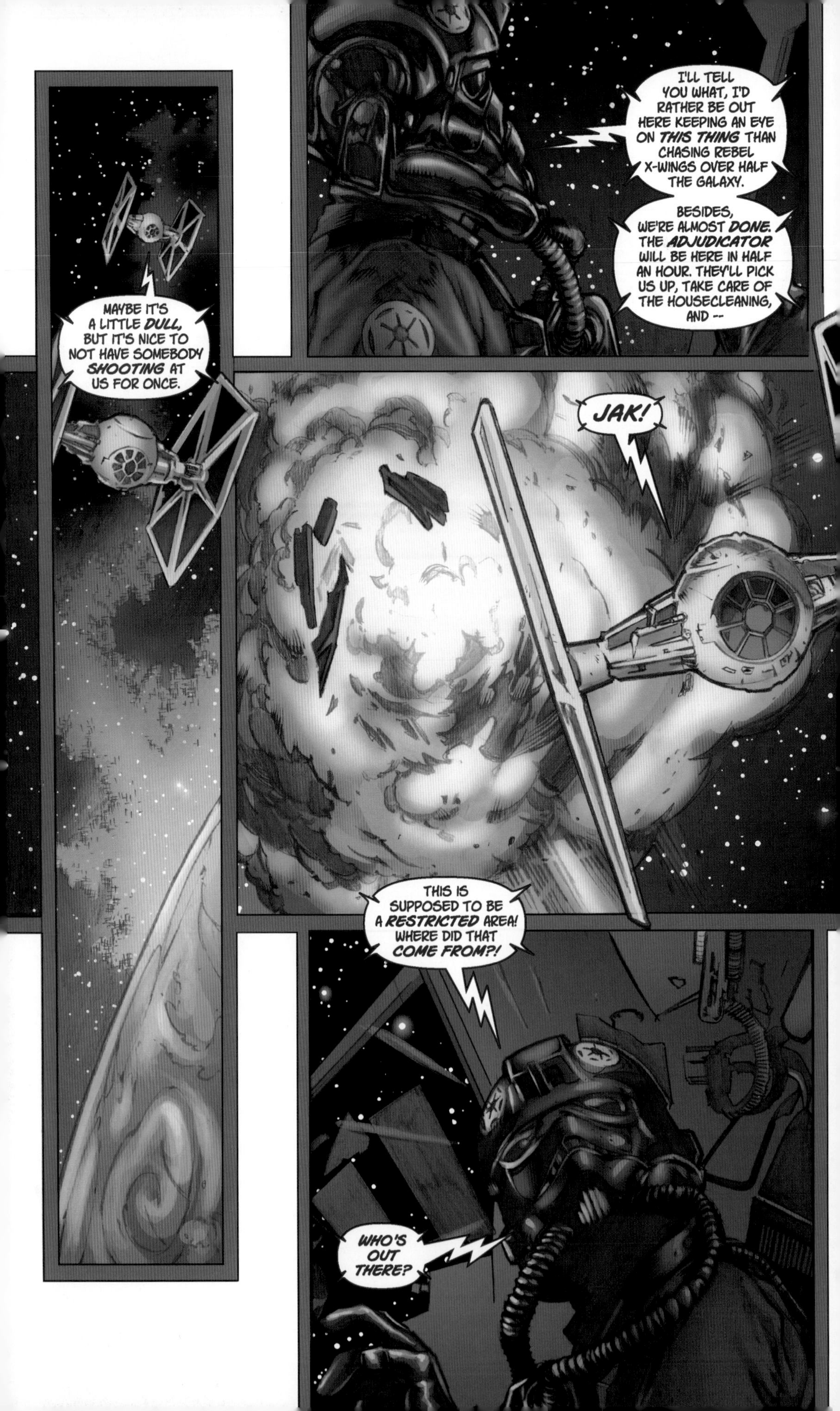
MAYBE IT'S A LITTLE DULL, BUT IT'S NICE TO NOT HAVE SOMEBODY SHOOTING AT US FOR ONCE.
I'LL TELL YOU WHAT, I'D RATHER BE OUT HERE KEEPING AN EYE ON THIS THING THAN CHASING REBEL X-WINGS OVER HALF THE GALAXY.
BESIDES, WE'RE ALMOST DONE. THE ADJUDICATOR WILL BE HERE IN HALF AN HOUR. THEY'LL PICK US UP, TAKE CARE OF THE HOUSECLEANING, AND --
JAK!
THIS IS SUPPOSED TO BE A RESTRICTED AREA! WHERE DID THAT COME FROM?!
WHO'S OUT THERE?

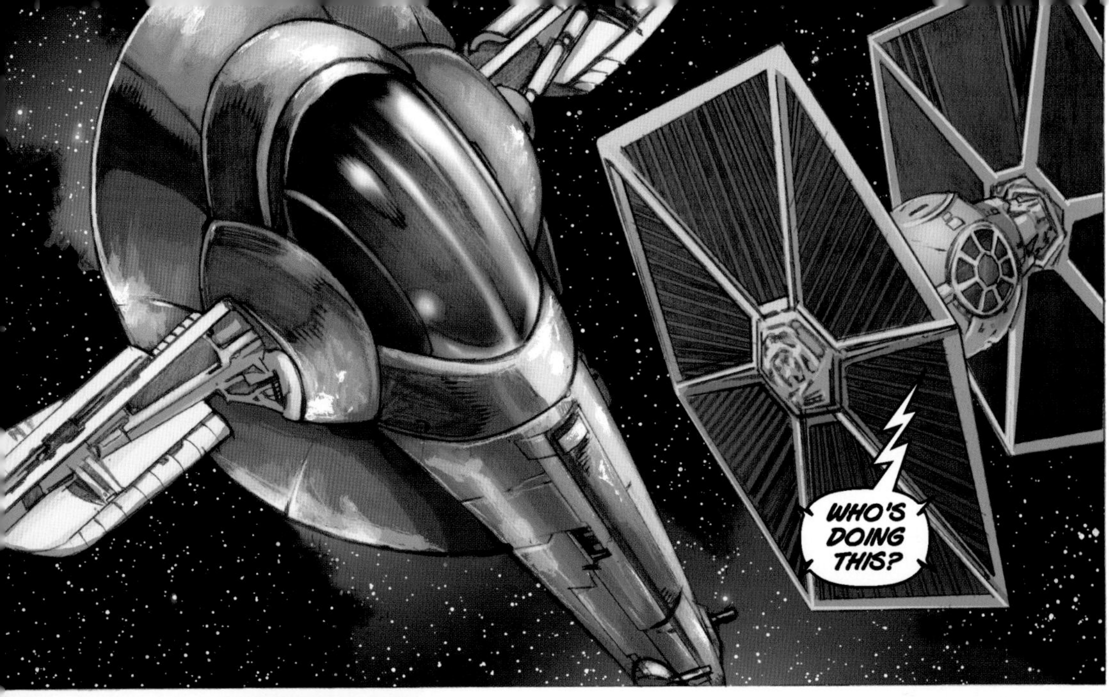
WHO'S DOING THIS?

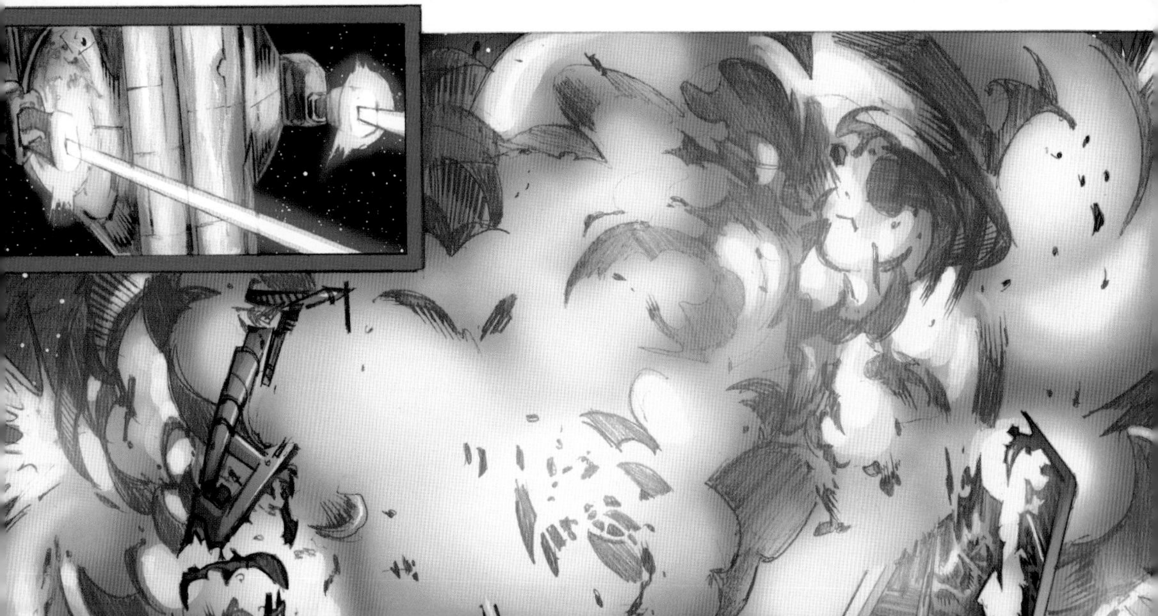

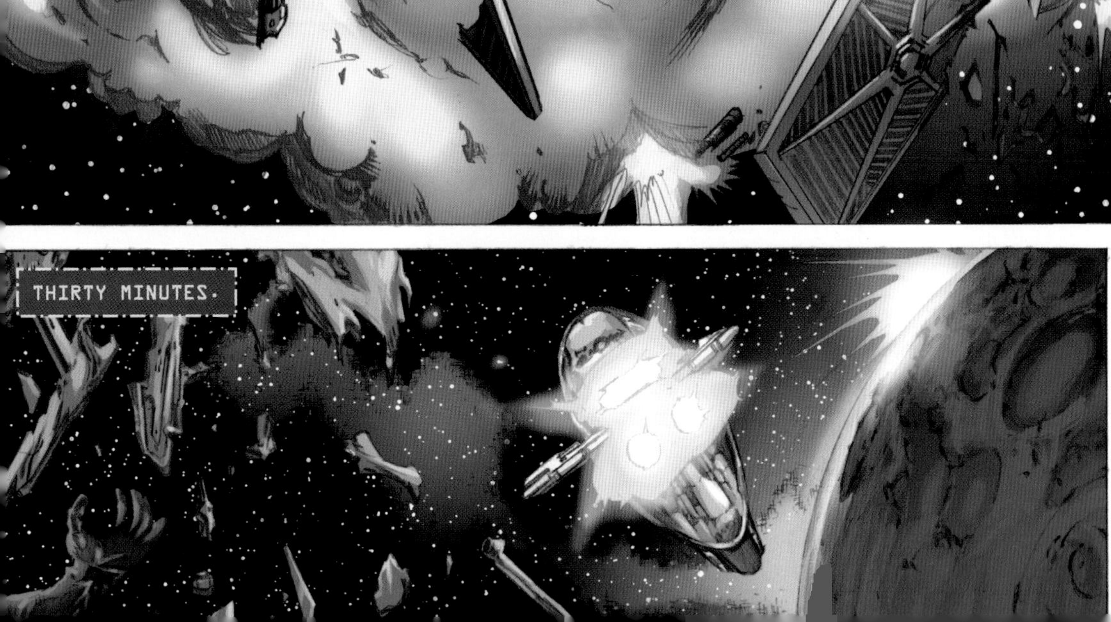
THIRTY MINUTES.

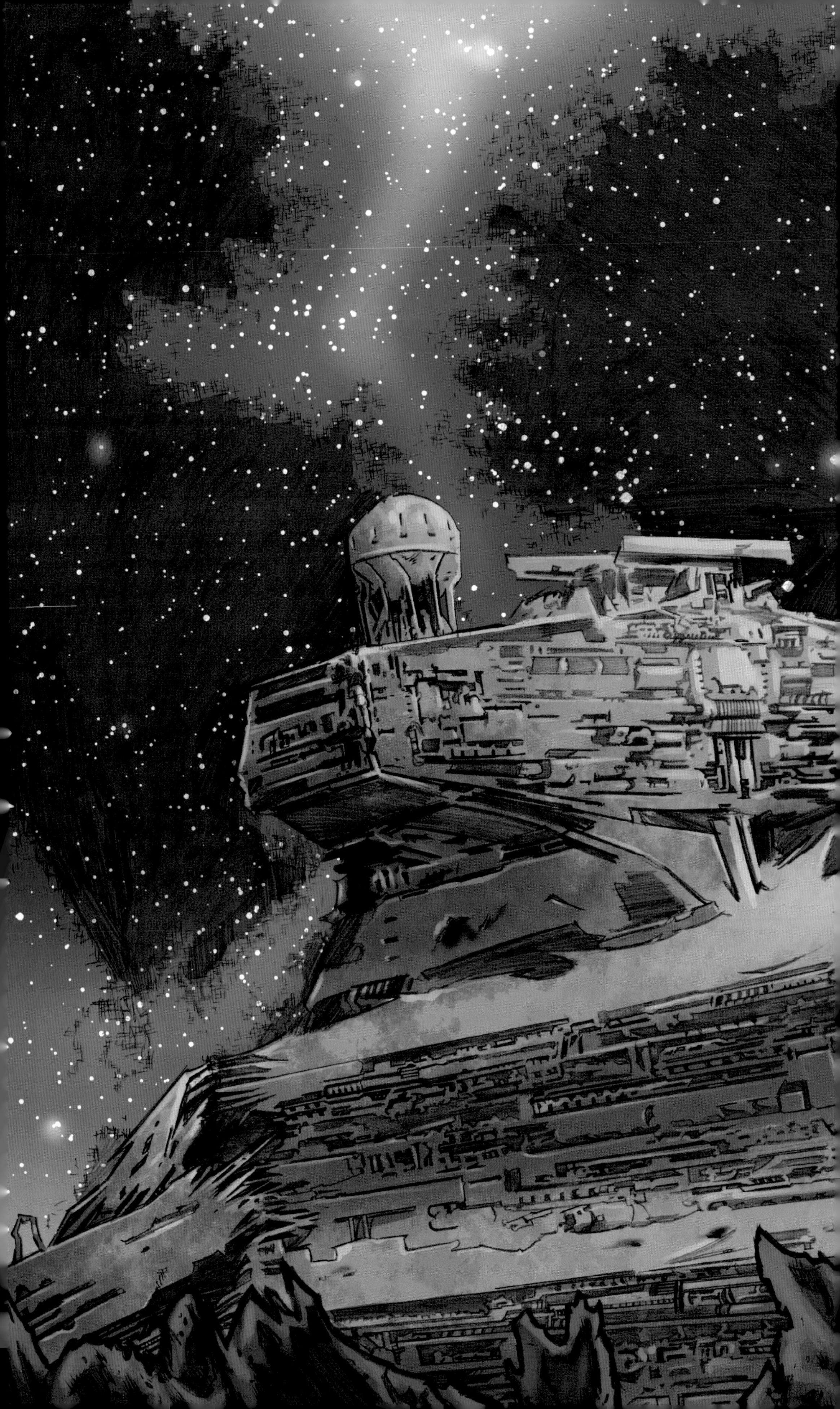

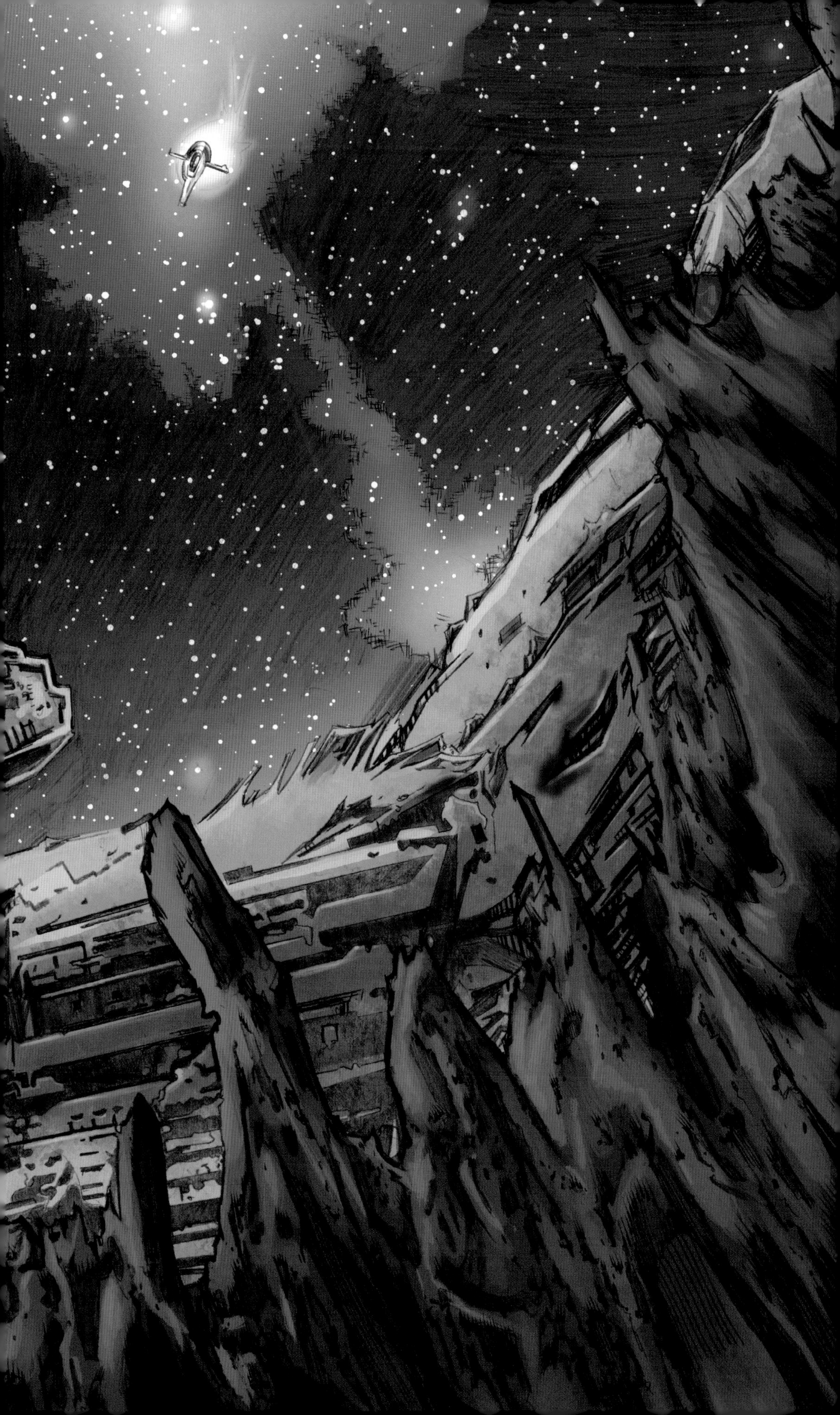

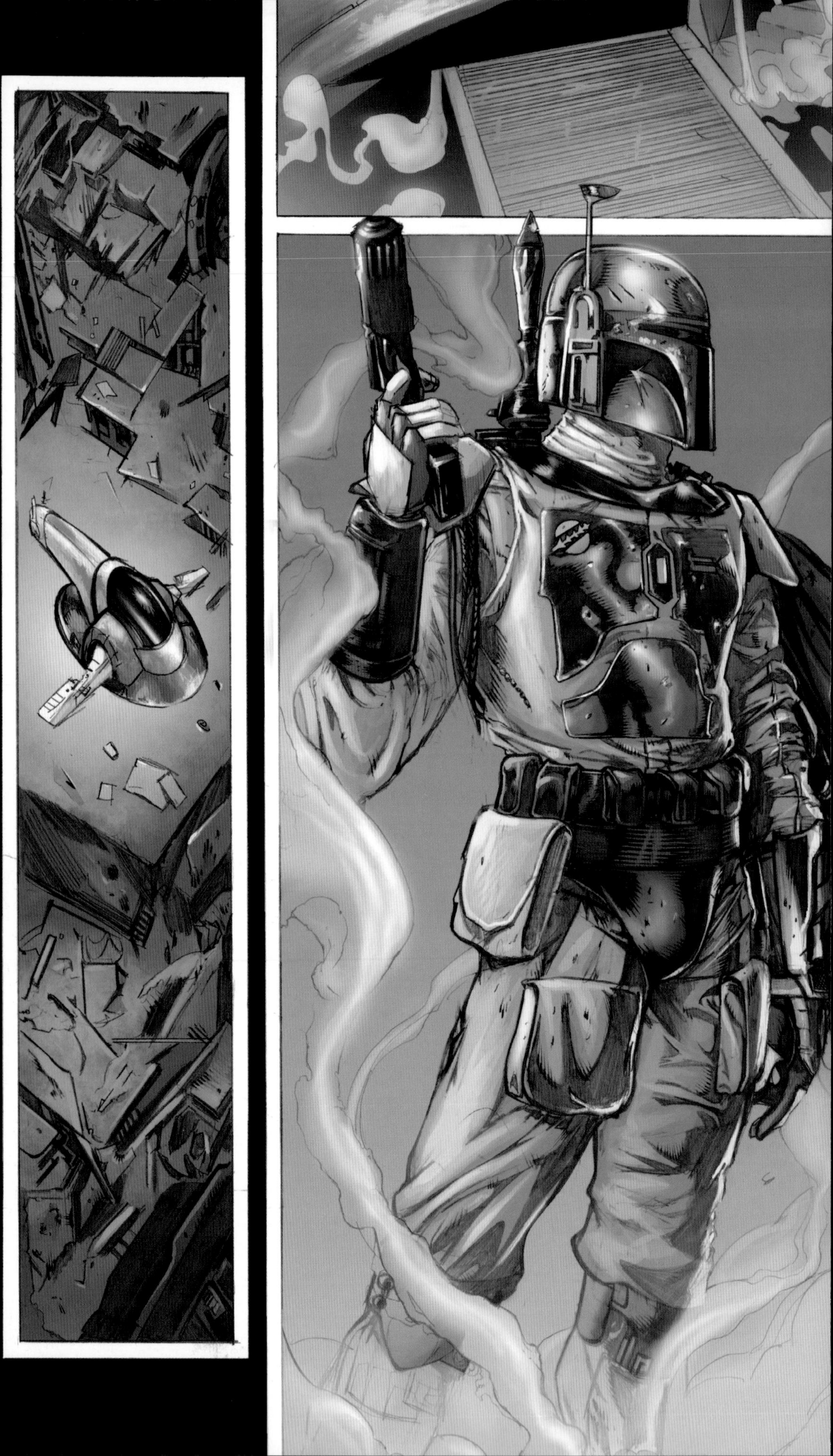

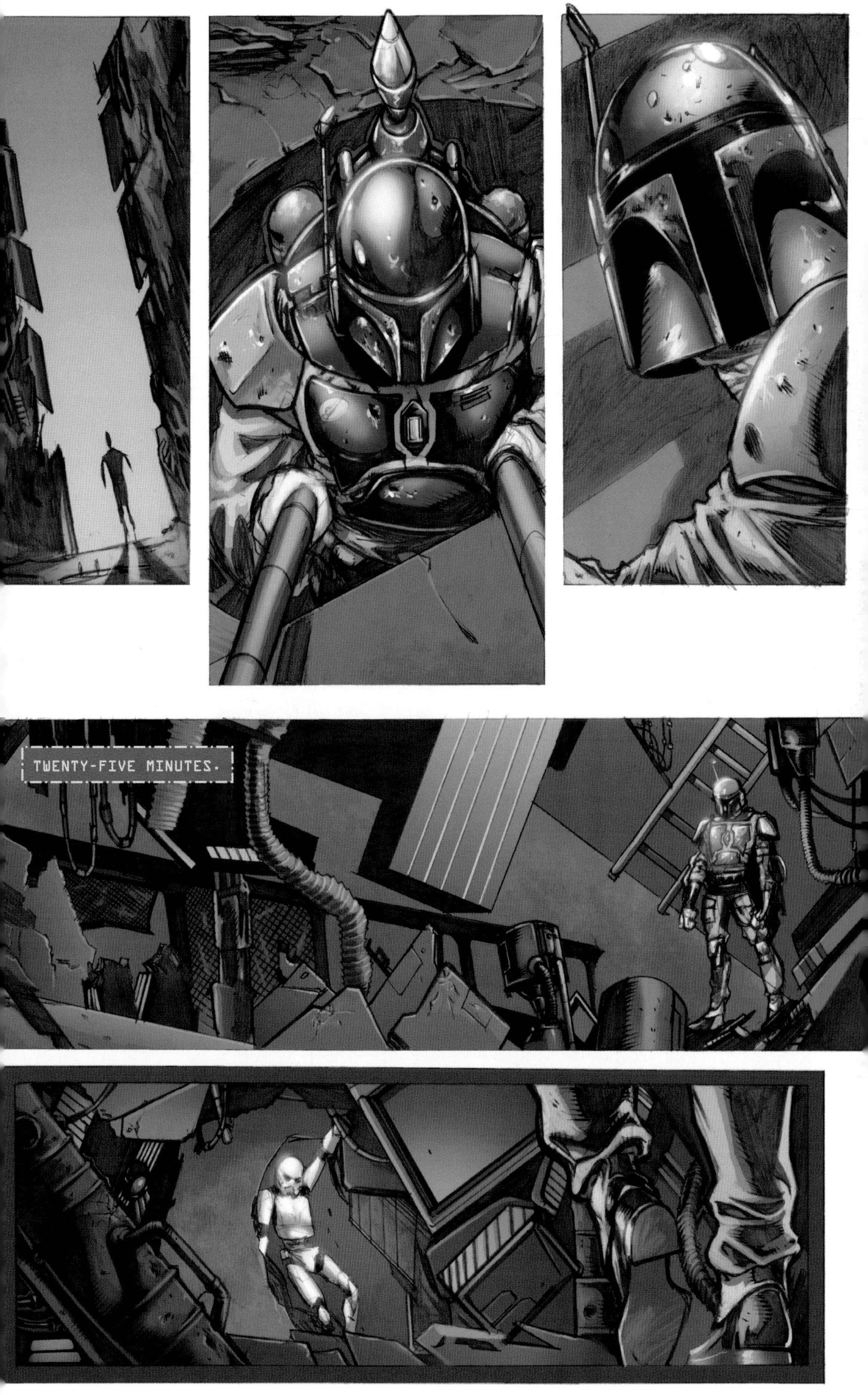
TWENTY-FIVE MINUTES.

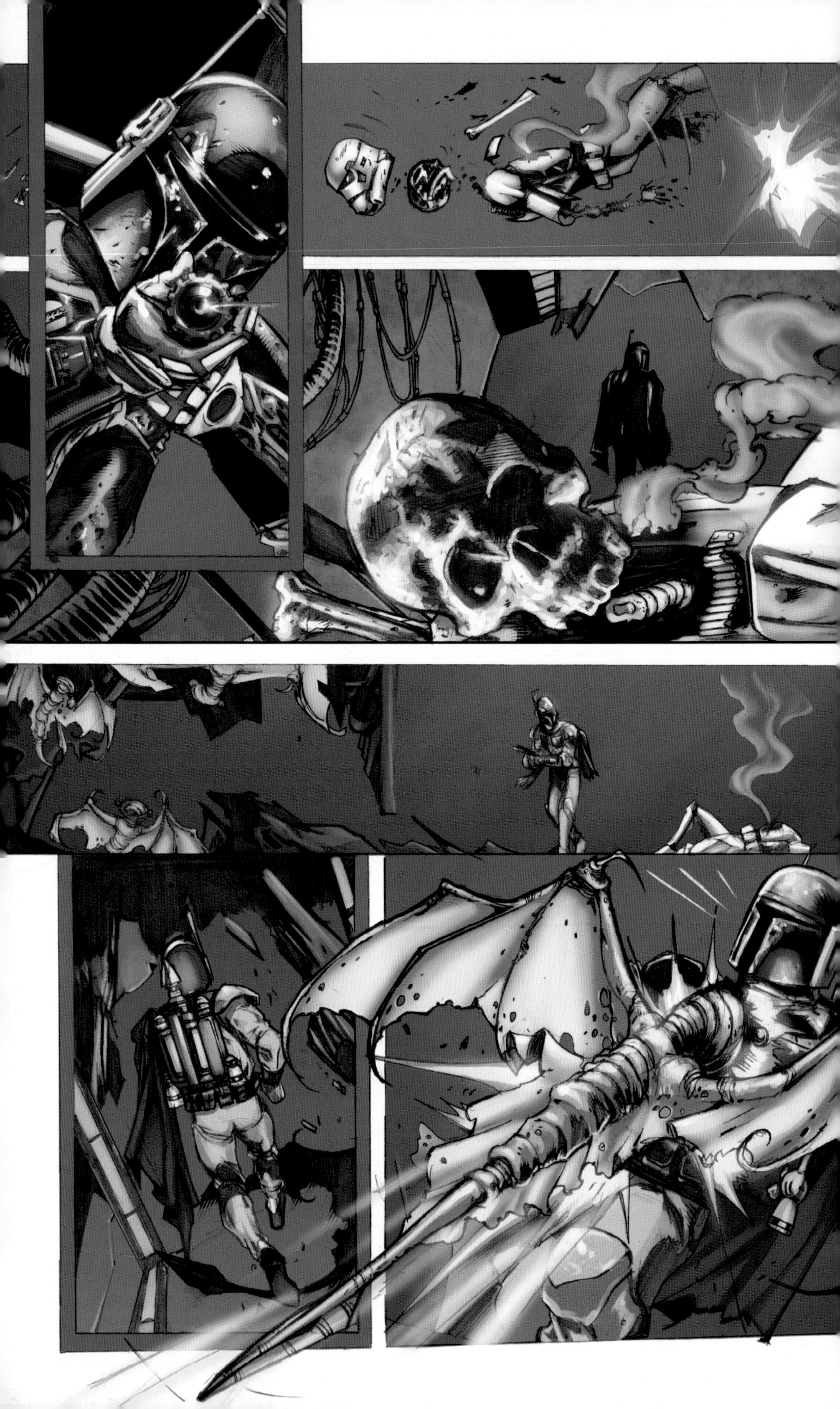

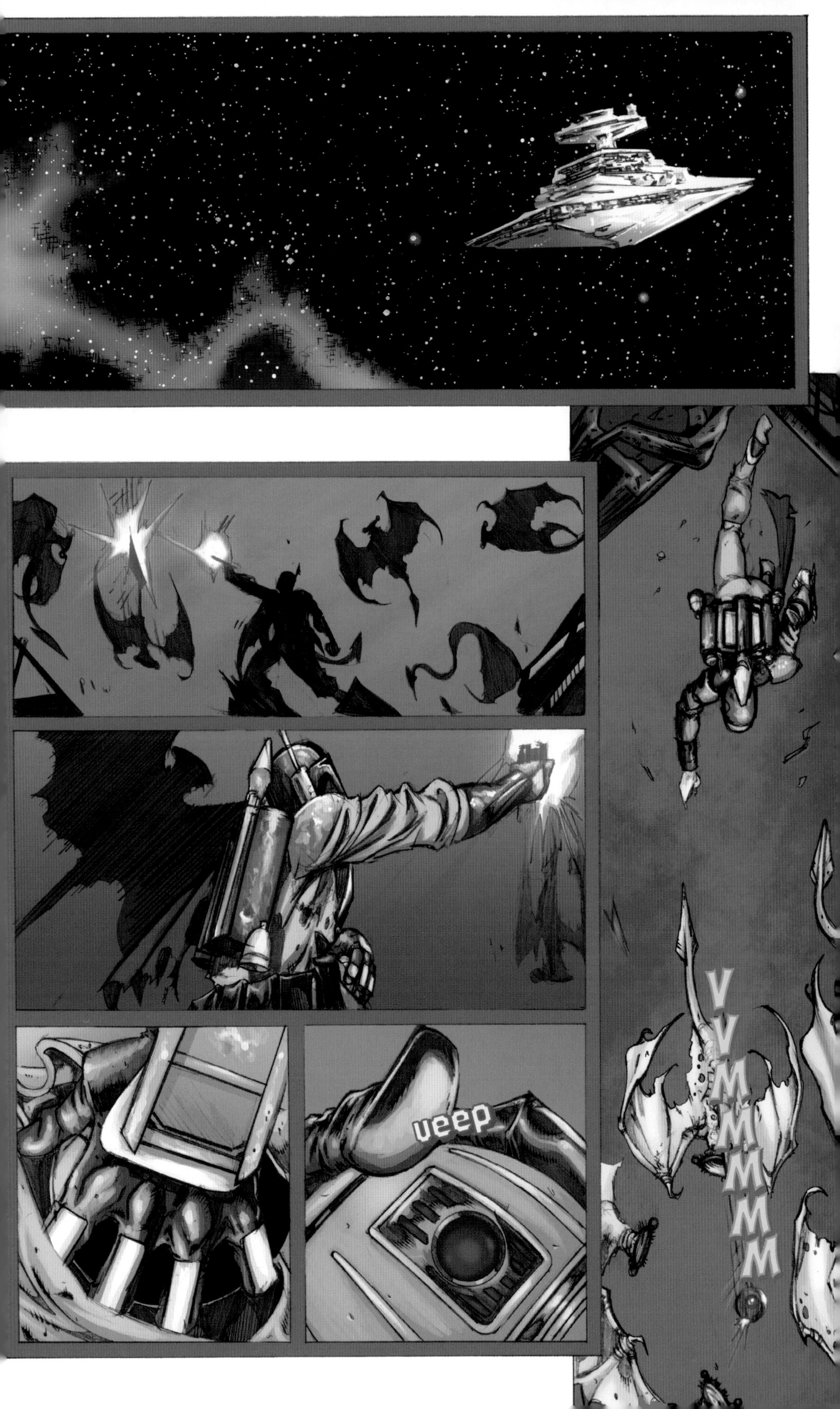
ueep
VVMMMMM

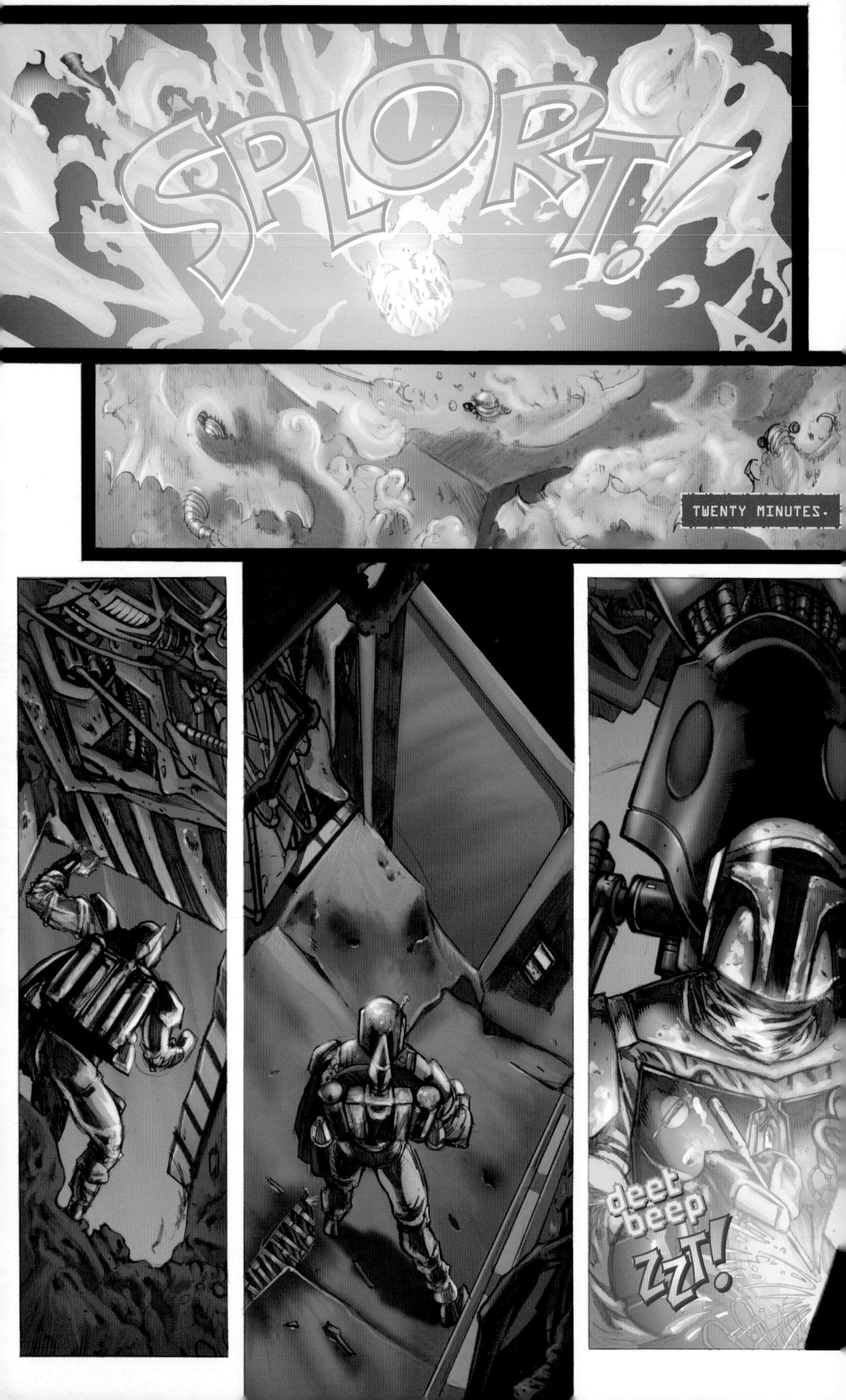
SPLORT!
TWENTY MINUTES.
deet beep
ZZT!

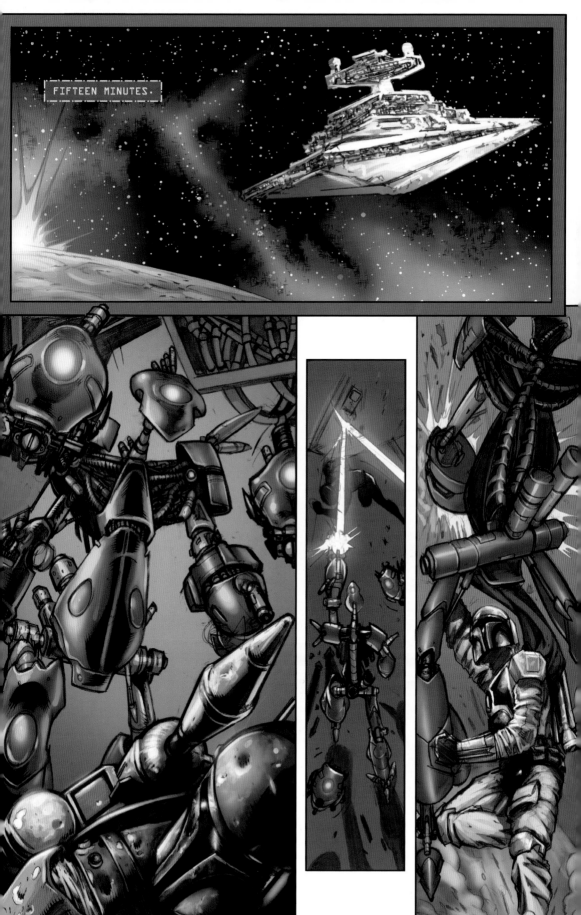

FIFTEEN MINUTES.

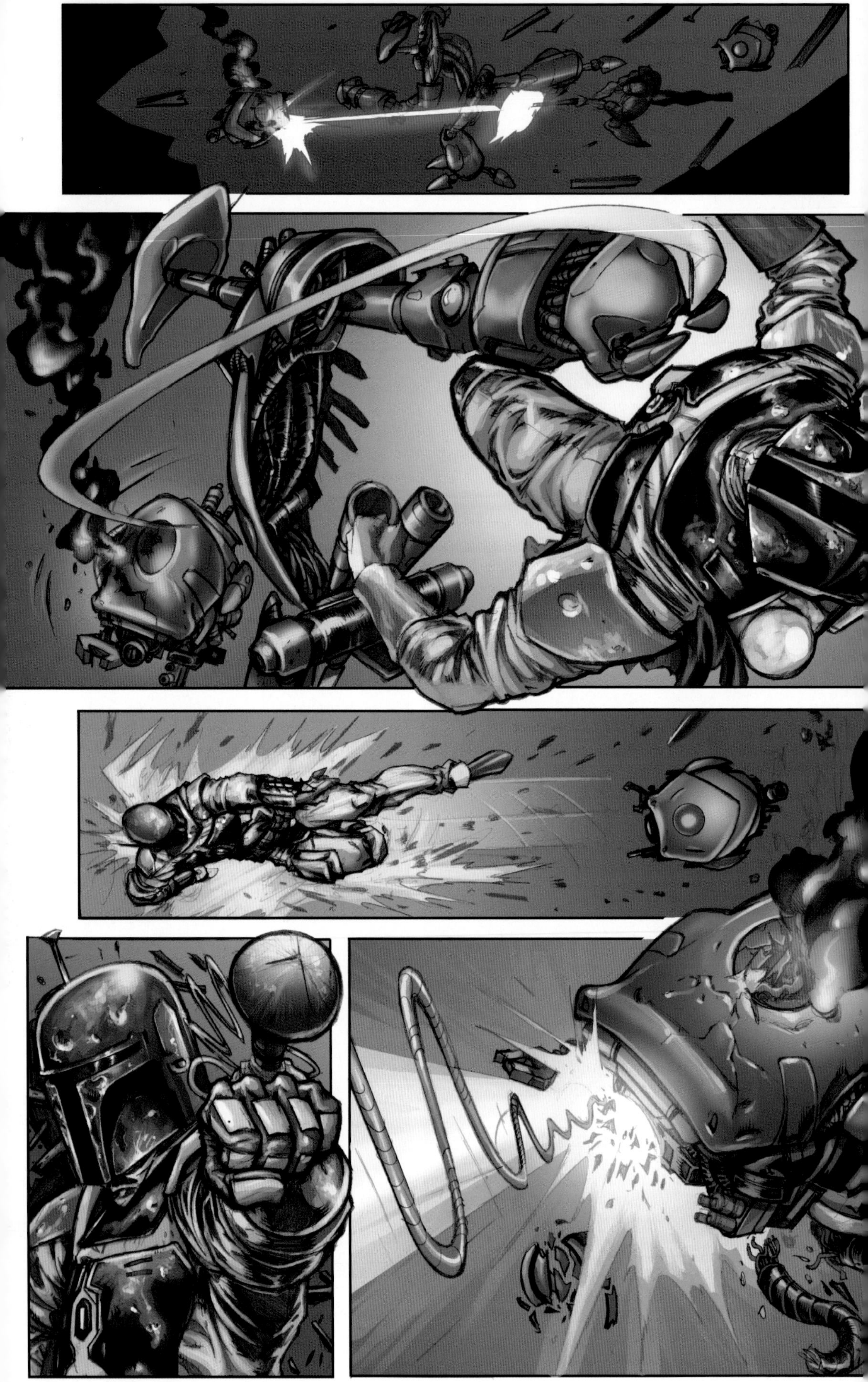

TEN MINUTES.

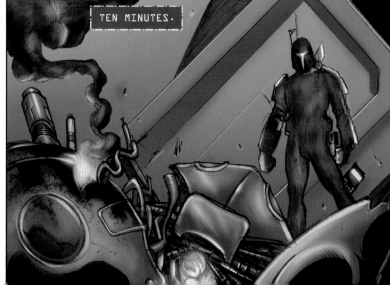

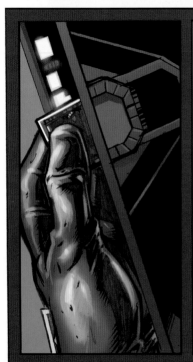

FIVE MINUTES.

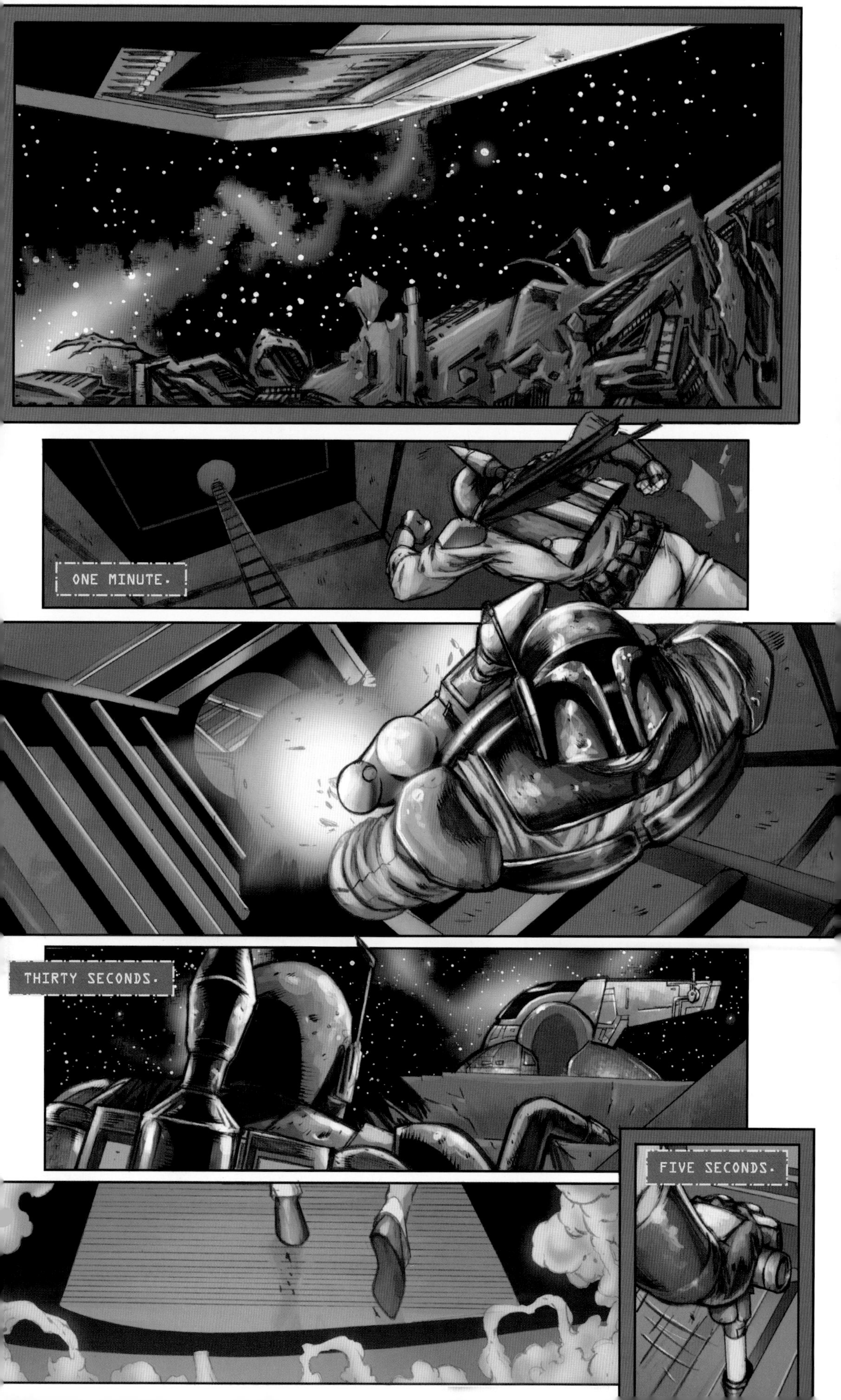
ONE MINUTE.
THIRTY SECONDS.
FIVE SECONDS.

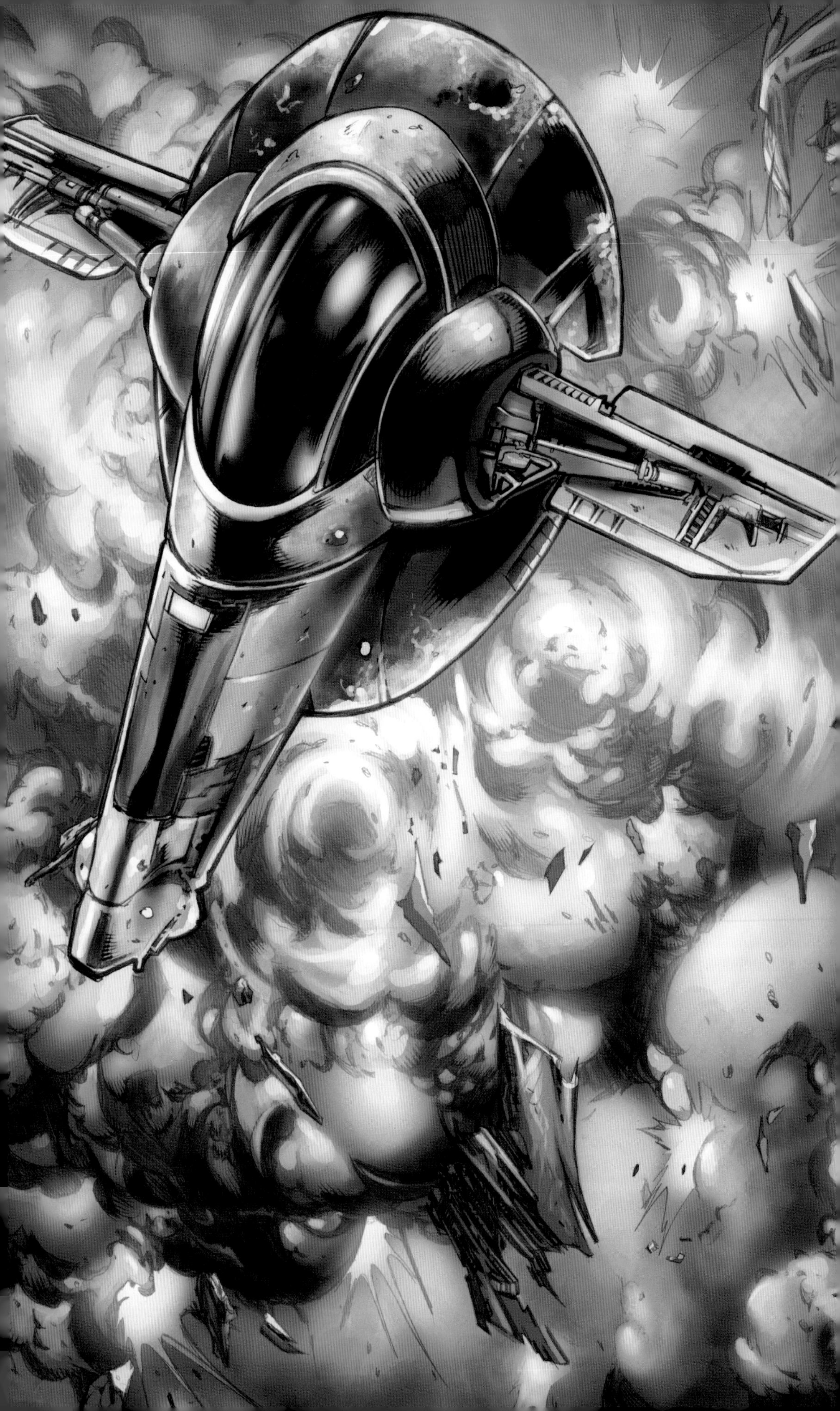

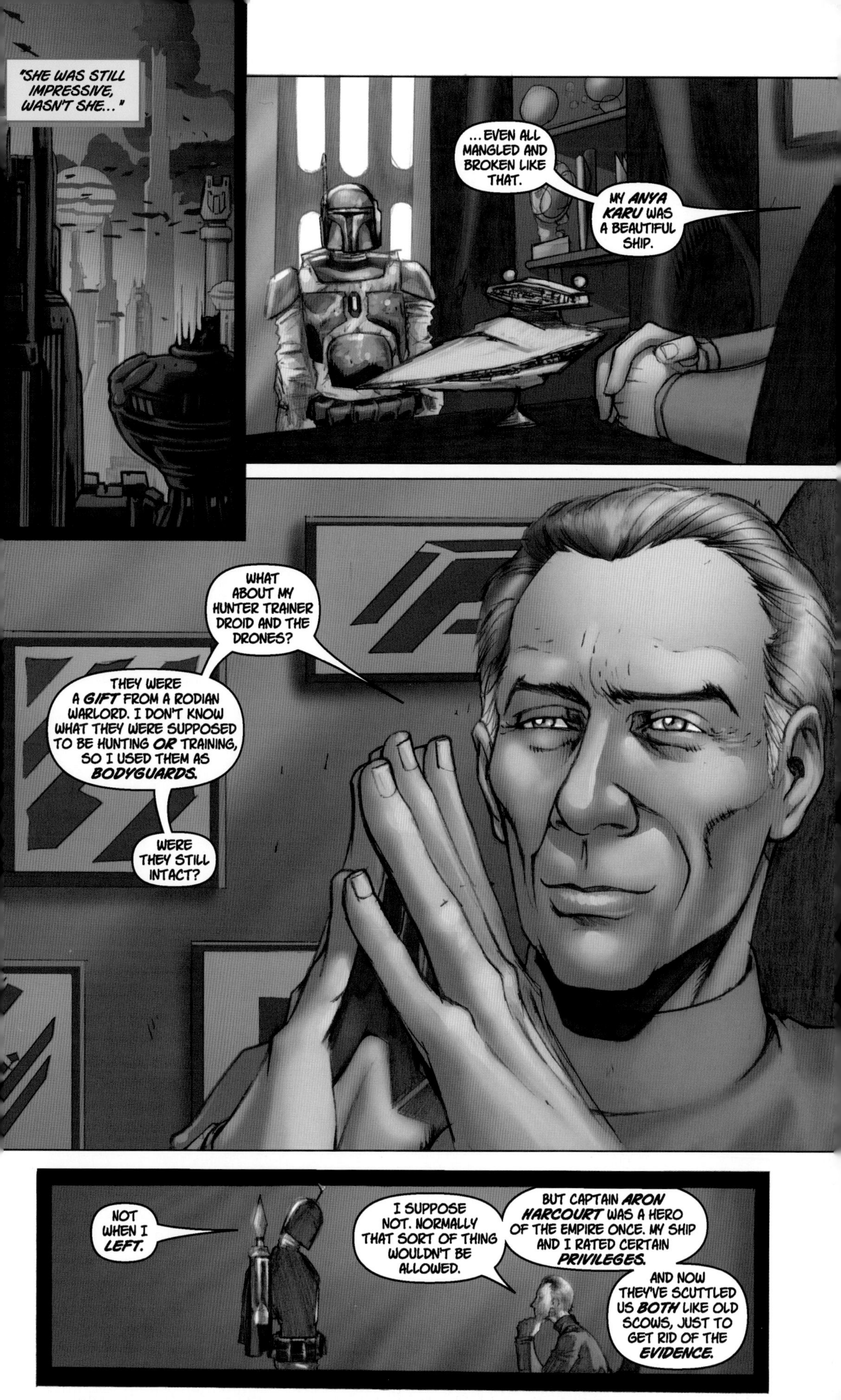
"SHE WAS STILL IMPRESSIVE, WASN'T SHE..."
...EVEN ALL MANGLED AND BROKEN LIKE THAT.
MY ANYA KARU WAS A BEAUTIFUL SHIP.
WHAT ABOUT MY HUNTER TRAINER DROID AND THE DRONES?
THEY WERE A GIFT FROM A RODIAN WARLORD. I DON'T KNOW WHAT THEY WERE SUPPOSED TO BE HUNTING OR TRAINING, SO I USED THEM AS BODYGUARDS.
WERE THEY STILL INTACT?
NOT WHEN I LEFT.
I SUPPOSE NOT. NORMALLY THAT SORT OF THING WOULDN'T BE ALLOWED.
BUT CAPTAIN ARON HARCOURT WAS A HERO OF THE EMPIRE ONCE. MY SHIP AND I RATED CERTAIN PRIVILEGES.
AND NOW THEY'VE SCUTTLED US BOTH LIKE OLD SCOWS, JUST TO GET RID OF THE EVIDENCE.

THEY BLAMED *ME* FOR THE *ANYA KARU* GOING DOWN, YOU KNOW. THE INQUIRY WAS FOR *SHOW.* BETTER TO FIND A *SCAPE-GOAT* --

-- EVEN ONE WITH THIRTY YEARS EXPERIENCE AS A COMMANDING OFFICER. THEY ENDED MY CAREER...

...RATHER THAN ADMIT THEY LOST ONE OF THEIR CAPITAL SHIPS...

...TO A TEAM OF *REBEL SABOTEURS.*

BUT ENOUGH OF AN OLD MAN'S REGRETS.

THE ITEM ... YOU *DID* GET IT, YES?

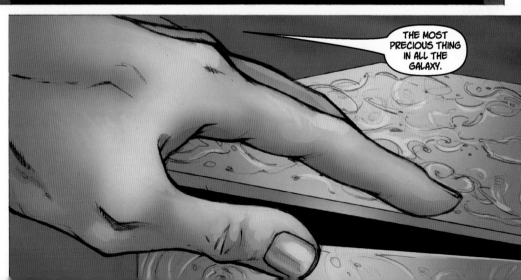

THE MOST PRECIOUS THING IN ALL THE GALAXY.

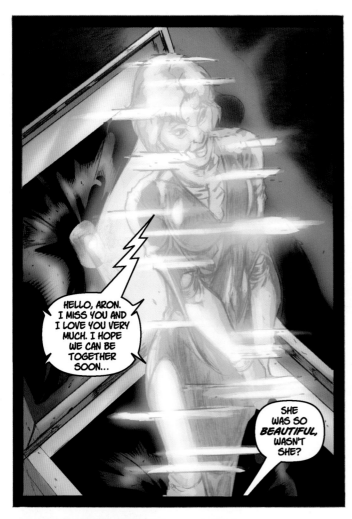

HELLO, ARON. I MISS YOU AND I LOVE YOU VERY MUCH. I HOPE WE CAN BE TOGETHER SOON...

SHE WAS SO *BEAUTIFUL*, WASN'T SHE?

WE MET WHILE I WAS STILL IN THE ACADEMY...

HELLO, ARON. I MISS YOU ...

SHE'S BEEN GONE MORE THAN THREE YEARS NOW.

SUCH A *SMALL* THING, BUT IT'S ALL I HAVE LEFT OF HER.

WHEN I GAVE THE ORDER TO ABANDON SHIP, THERE WAS NO TIME TO GO BACK FOR HER.

BUT I KNEW IF ANYONE IN THE GALAXY COULD BRING HER TO ME, IT WOULD BE *BOBA FETT*.

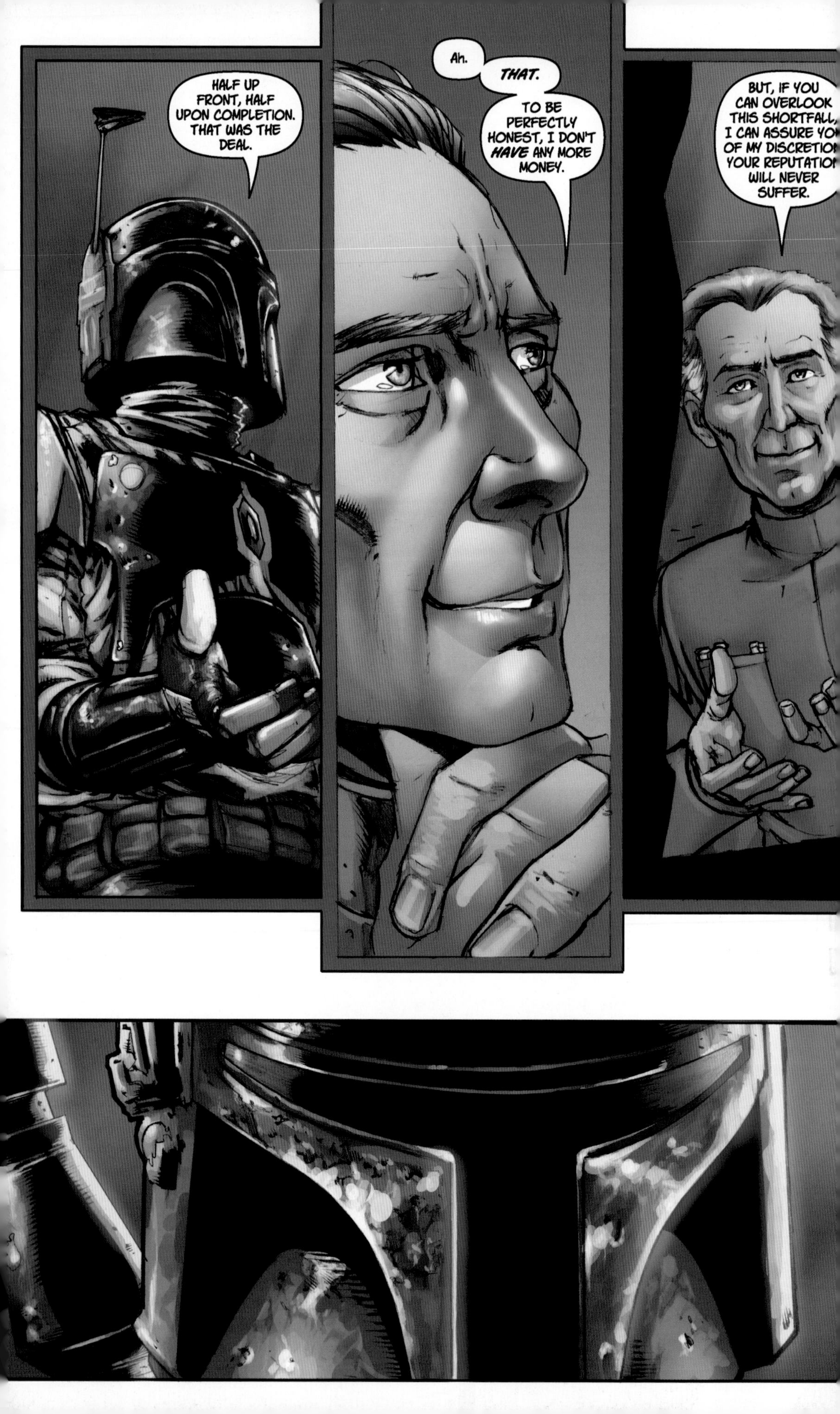
HALF UP FRONT, HALF UPON COMPLETION. THAT WAS THE DEAL.
Ah.
THAT.
TO BE PERFECTLY HONEST, I DON'T HAVE ANY MORE MONEY.
BUT, IF YOU CAN OVERLOOK THIS SHORTFALL, I CAN ASSURE YO OF MY DISCRETIO YOUR REPUTATIO WILL NEVER SUFFER.

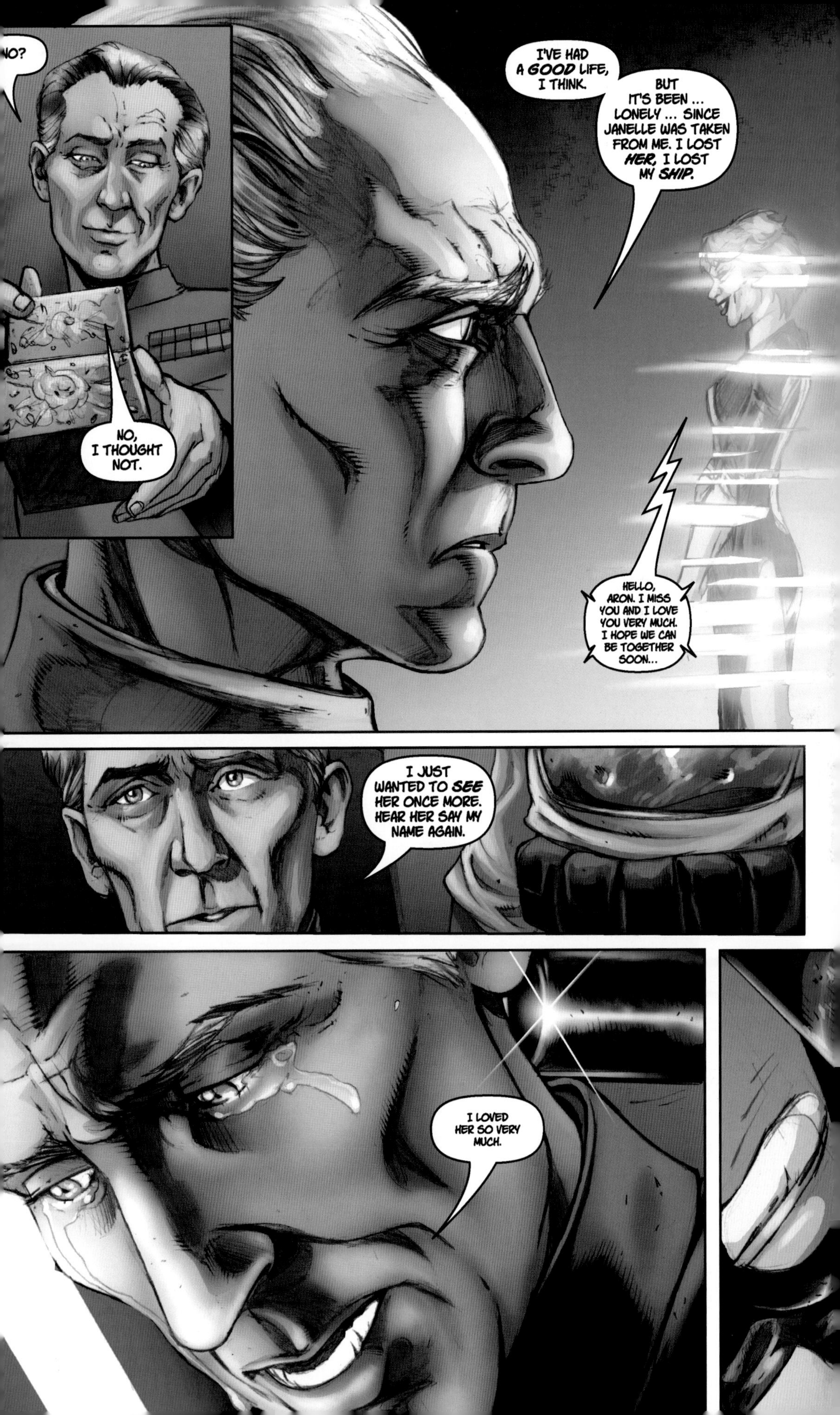
NO?
NO, I THOUGHT NOT.
I'VE HAD A GOOD LIFE, I THINK.
BUT IT'S BEEN ... LONELY ... SINCE JANELLE WAS TAKEN FROM ME. I LOST HER, I LOST MY SHIP.
HELLO, ARON. I MISS YOU AND I LOVE YOU VERY MUCH. I HOPE WE CAN BE TOGETHER SOON...
I JUST WANTED TO SEE HER ONCE MORE. HEAR HER SAY MY NAME AGAIN.
I LOVED HER SO VERY MUCH.

END

Illustration by Adam Hughes

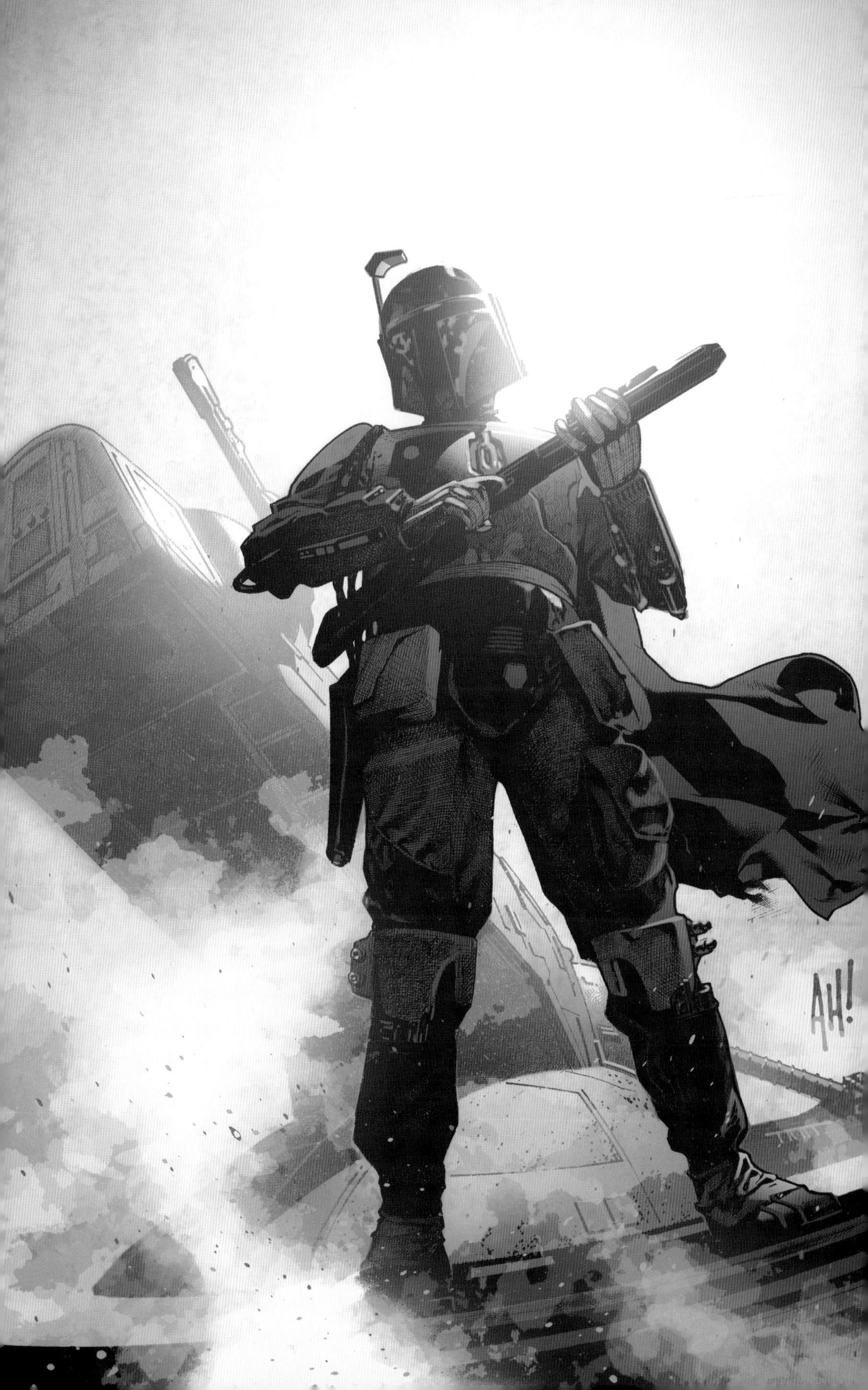

AH!

OVERKILL

SCRIPT
Thomas Andrews

ART and COLORS
Francisco Ruiz Velasco

LETTERS
Michael David Thomas

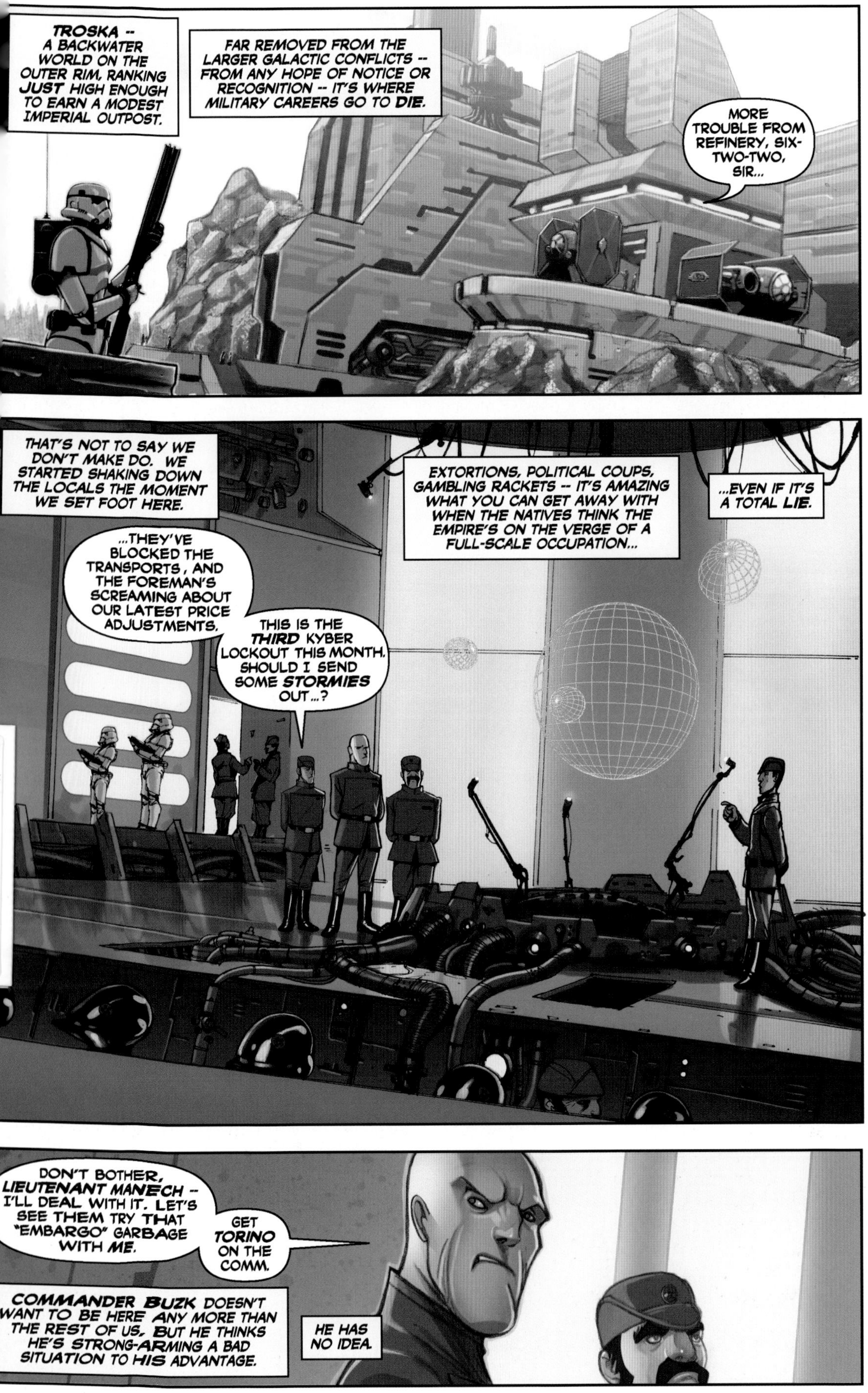
TROSKA -- A BACKWATER WORLD ON THE OUTER RIM, RANKING JUST HIGH ENOUGH TO EARN A MODEST IMPERIAL OUTPOST.
FAR REMOVED FROM THE LARGER GALACTIC CONFLICTS -- FROM ANY HOPE OF NOTICE OR RECOGNITION -- IT'S WHERE MILITARY CAREERS GO TO DIE.
MORE TROUBLE FROM REFINERY, SIX-TWO-TWO, SIR...
THAT'S NOT TO SAY WE DON'T MAKE DO. WE STARTED SHAKING DOWN THE LOCALS THE MOMENT WE SET FOOT HERE.
EXTORTIONS, POLITICAL COUPS, GAMBLING RACKETS -- IT'S AMAZING WHAT YOU CAN GET AWAY WITH WHEN THE NATIVES THINK THE EMPIRE'S ON THE VERGE OF A FULL-SCALE OCCUPATION...
...EVEN IF IT'S A TOTAL LIE.
...THEY'VE BLOCKED THE TRANSPORTS, AND THE FOREMAN'S SCREAMING ABOUT OUR LATEST PRICE ADJUSTMENTS.
THIS IS THE THIRD KYBER LOCKOUT THIS MONTH. SHOULD I SEND SOME STORMIES OUT...?
DON'T BOTHER, LIEUTENANT MANECH -- I'LL DEAL WITH IT. LET'S SEE THEM TRY THAT "EMBARGO" GARBAGE WITH ME.
GET TORINO ON THE COMM.
COMMANDER BUZK DOESN'T WANT TO BE HERE ANY MORE THAN THE REST OF US, BUT HE THINKS HE'S STRONG-ARMING A BAD SITUATION TO HIS ADVANTAGE.
HE HAS NO IDEA.

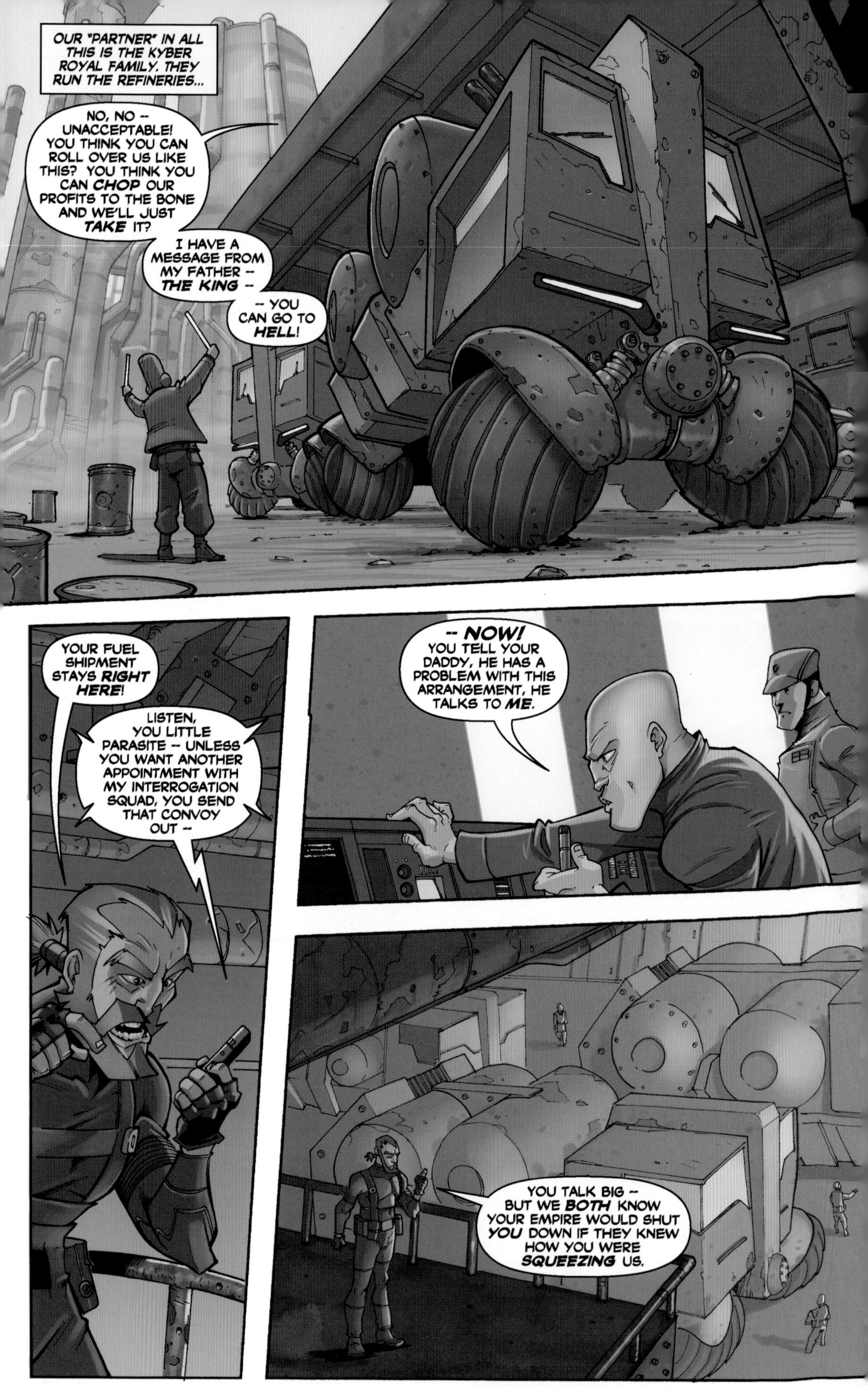
OUR "PARTNER" IN ALL THIS IS THE KYBER ROYAL FAMILY. THEY RUN THE REFINERIES...
NO, NO -- UNACCEPTABLE! YOU THINK YOU CAN ROLL OVER US LIKE THIS? YOU THINK YOU CAN CHOP OUR PROFITS TO THE BONE AND WE'LL JUST TAKE IT?
I HAVE A MESSAGE FROM MY FATHER -- THE KING --
-- YOU CAN GO TO HELL!
YOUR FUEL SHIPMENT STAYS RIGHT HERE!
LISTEN, YOU LITTLE PARASITE -- UNLESS YOU WANT ANOTHER APPOINTMENT WITH MY INTERROGATION SQUAD, YOU SEND THAT CONVOY OUT --
-- NOW! YOU TELL YOUR DADDY, HE HAS A PROBLEM WITH THIS ARRANGEMENT, HE TALKS TO ME.
YOU TALK BIG -- BUT WE BOTH KNOW YOUR EMPIRE WOULD SHUT YOU DOWN IF THEY KNEW HOW YOU WERE SQUEEZING US.

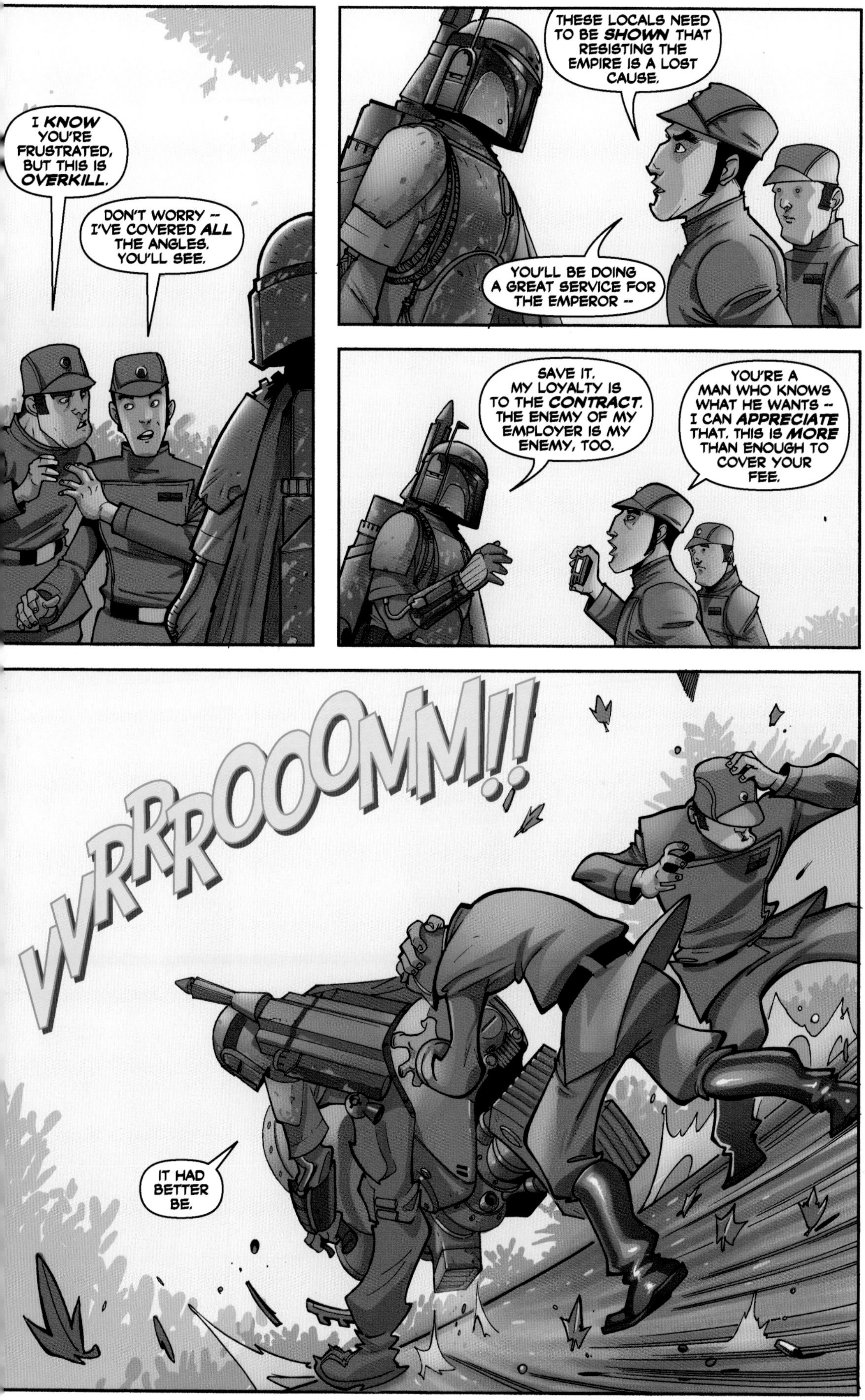
I KNOW YOU'RE FRUSTRATED, BUT THIS IS OVERKILL.
DON'T WORRY -- I'VE COVERED ALL THE ANGLES. YOU'LL SEE.
THESE LOCALS NEED TO BE SHOWN THAT RESISTING THE EMPIRE IS A LOST CAUSE.
YOU'LL BE DOING A GREAT SERVICE FOR THE EMPEROR --
SAVE IT. MY LOYALTY IS TO THE CONTRACT. THE ENEMY OF MY EMPLOYER IS MY ENEMY, TOO.
YOU'RE A MAN WHO KNOWS WHAT HE WANTS -- I CAN APPRECIATE THAT. THIS IS MORE THAN ENOUGH TO COVER YOUR FEE.
VVRRROOOMM!!
IT HAD BETTER BE.

WE ARE SO DEAD RIGHT NOW.

KELMONT, MY FRIEND -- *THAT* IS HOW YOU GET THINGS DONE.

YOU'VE JUST WITNESSED THE BEGINNING OF A LONG AND *EXCEPTIONAL* MILITARY CAREER.

OH, COME ON ... SO SOME KYBERS GET *KNOCKED AROUND* A LITTLE. BOBA FETT'S A PROFESSIONAL -- HE KNOWS WHAT HE'S DOING...

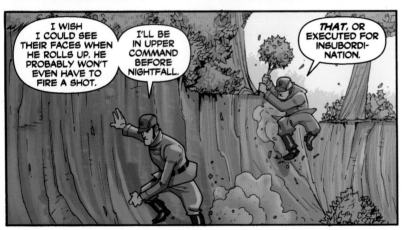

I WISH I COULD SEE THEIR FACES WHEN HE ROLLS UP. HE PROBABLY WON'T EVEN HAVE TO FIRE A SHOT.

I'LL BE IN UPPER COMMAND BEFORE NIGHTFALL.

THAT, OR EXECUTED FOR INSUBORDI- NATION.

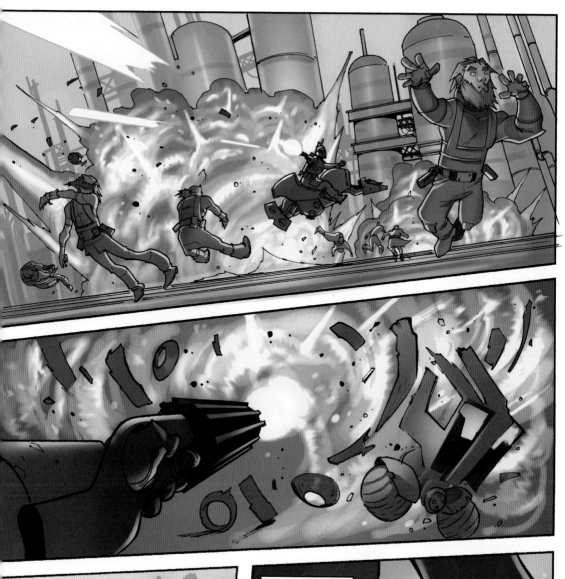

"...WHAT'S THE WORST THAT COULD HAPPEN?"

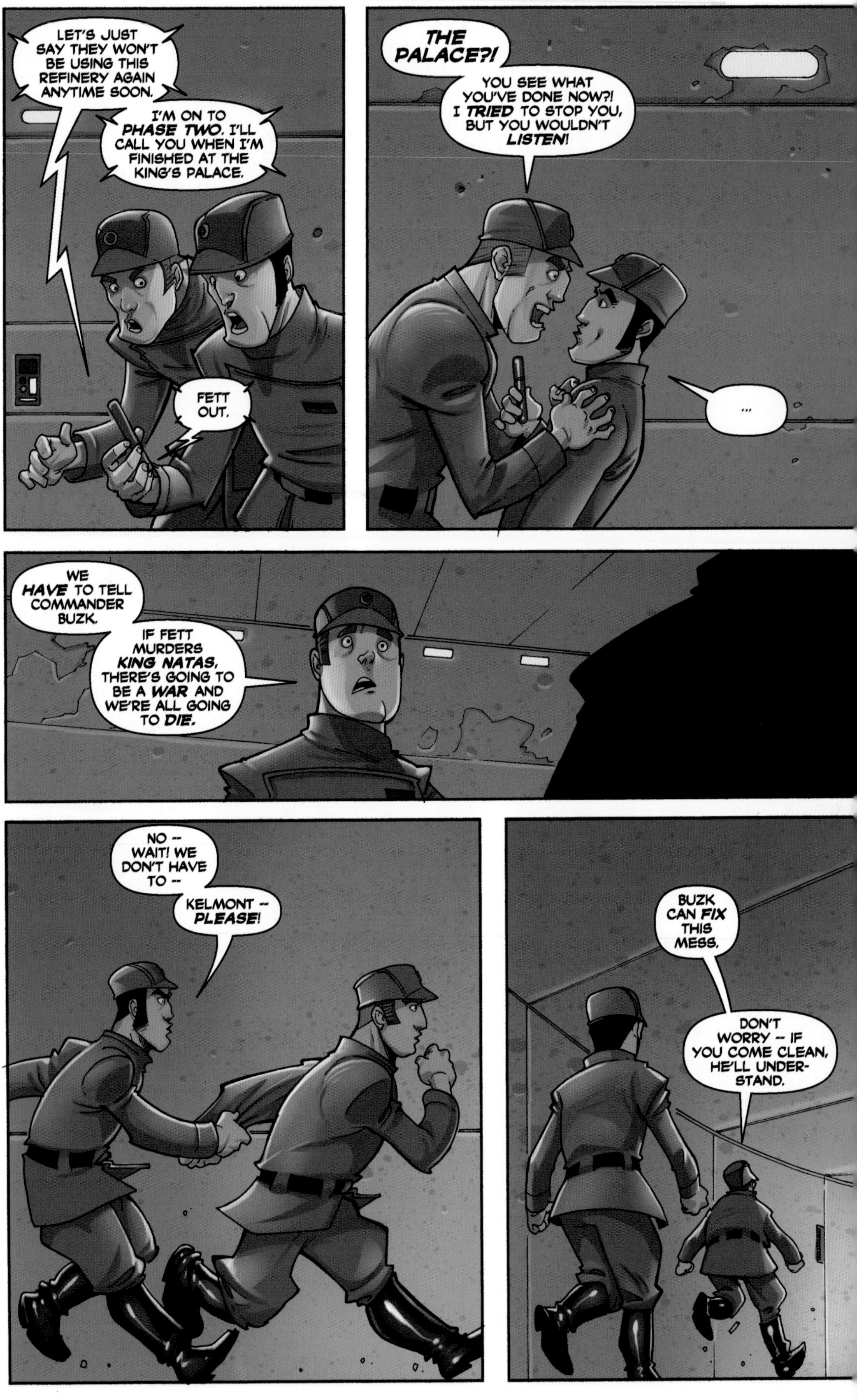
LET'S JUST SAY THEY WON'T BE USING THIS REFINERY AGAIN ANYTIME SOON.
I'M ON TO PHASE TWO. I'LL CALL YOU WHEN I'M FINISHED AT THE KING'S PALACE.
FETT OUT.
THE PALACE?!
YOU SEE WHAT YOU'VE DONE NOW?! I TRIED TO STOP YOU, BUT YOU WOULDN'T LISTEN!
...
WE HAVE TO TELL COMMANDER BUZK.
IF FETT MURDERS KING NATAS, THERE'S GOING TO BE A WAR AND WE'RE ALL GOING TO DIE.
NO -- WAIT! WE DON'T HAVE TO --
KELMONT -- PLEASE!
BUZK CAN FIX THIS MESS.
DON'T WORRY -- IF YOU COME CLEAN, HE'LL UNDER-STAND.

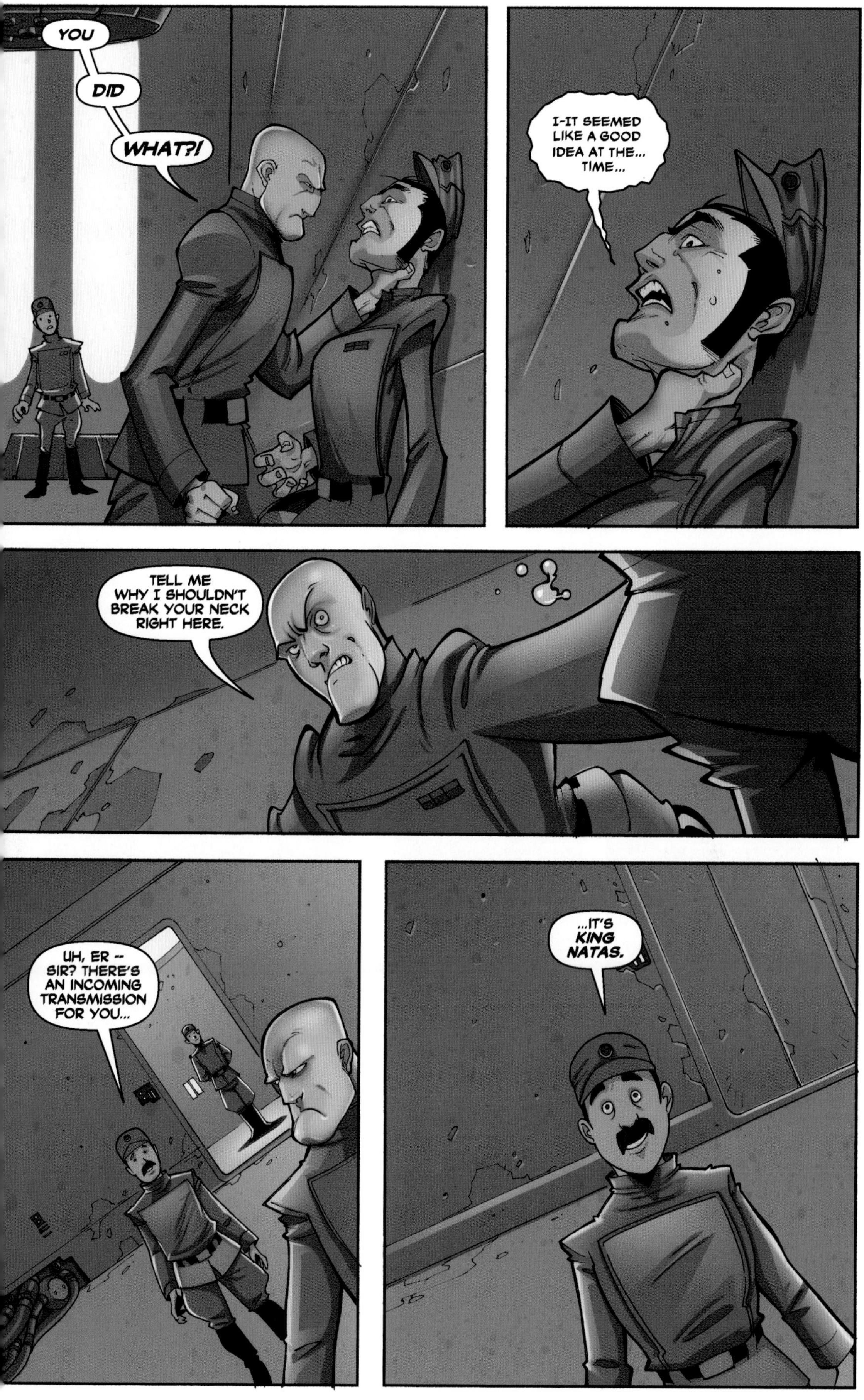
YOU
DID
WHAT?!
I-IT SEEMED LIKE A GOOD IDEA AT THE... TIME...
TELL ME WHY I SHOULDN'T BREAK YOUR NECK RIGHT HERE.
UH, ER -- SIR? THERE'S AN INCOMING TRANSMISSION FOR YOU...
...IT'S KING NATAS.

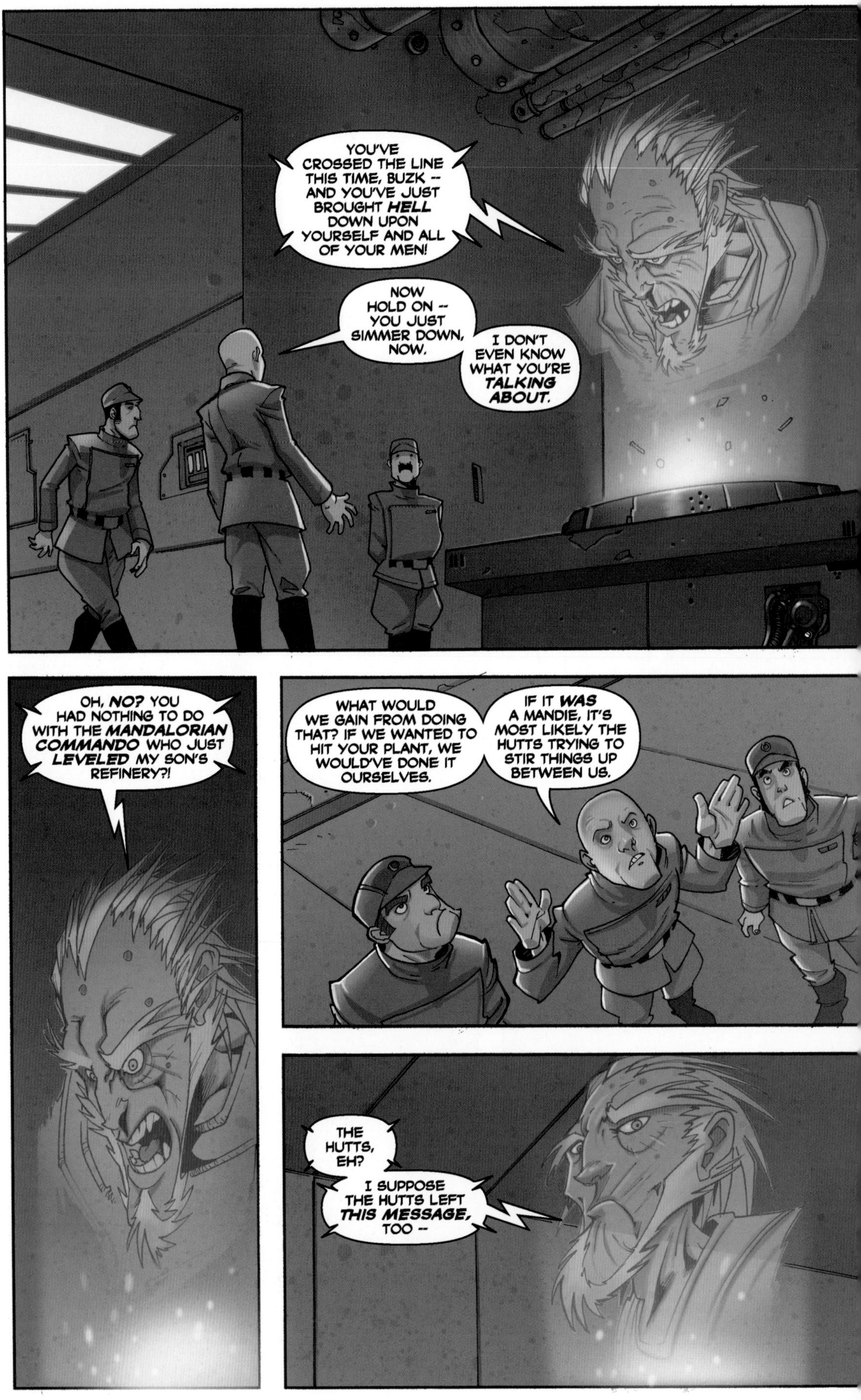
YOU'VE CROSSED THE LINE THIS TIME, BUZK -- AND YOU'VE JUST BROUGHT HELL DOWN UPON YOURSELF AND ALL OF YOUR MEN!
NOW HOLD ON -- YOU JUST SIMMER DOWN, NOW.
I DON'T EVEN KNOW WHAT YOU'RE TALKING ABOUT.
OH, NO? YOU HAD NOTHING TO DO WITH THE MANDALORIAN COMMANDO WHO JUST LEVELED MY SON'S REFINERY?!
WHAT WOULD WE GAIN FROM DOING THAT? IF WE WANTED TO HIT YOUR PLANT, WE WOULD'VE DONE IT OURSELVES.
IF IT WAS A MANDIE, IT'S MOST LIKELY THE HUTTS TRYING TO STIR THINGS UP BETWEEN US.
THE HUTTS, EH?
I SUPPOSE THE HUTTS LEFT THIS MESSAGE, TOO --

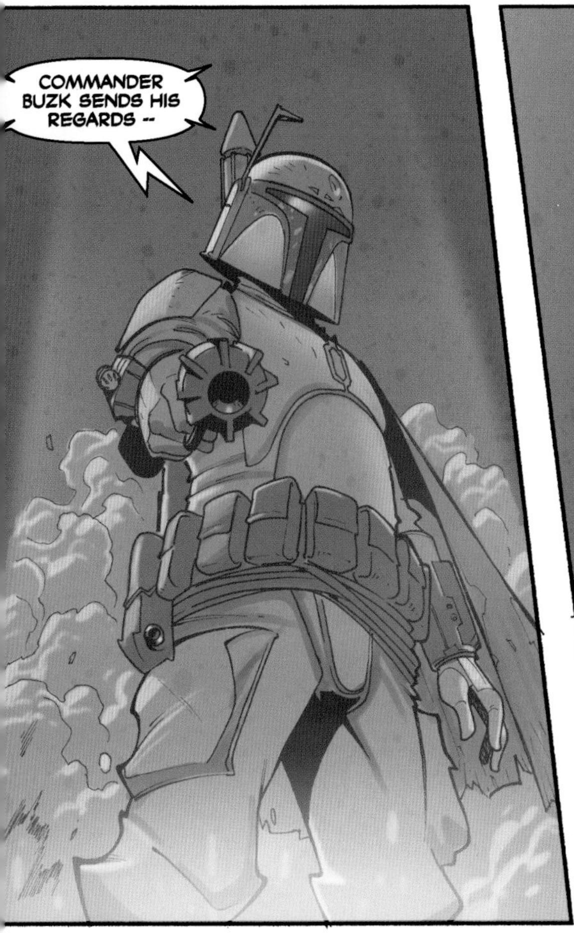
COMMANDER BUZK SENDS HIS REGARDS --

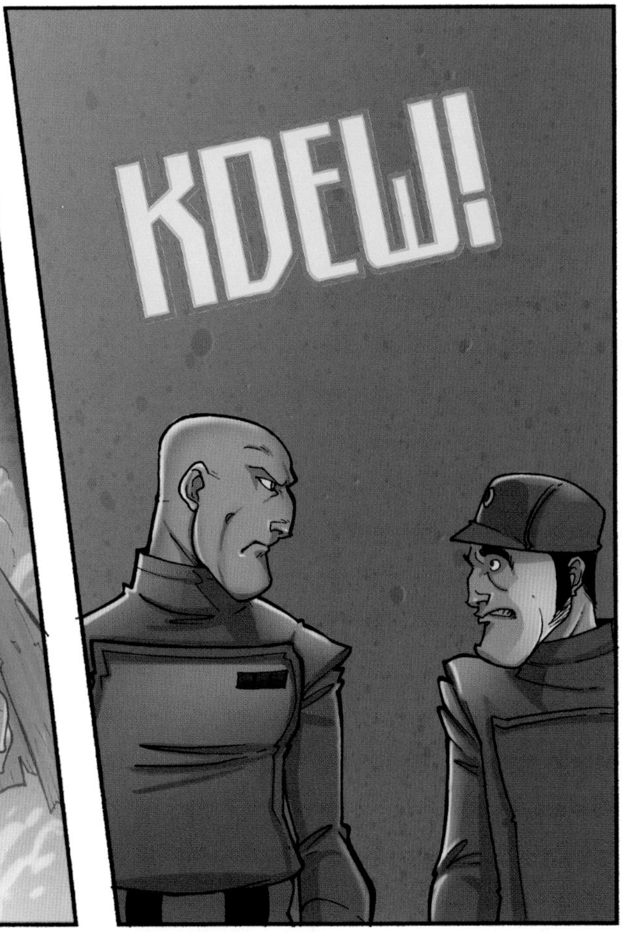
KDEW!

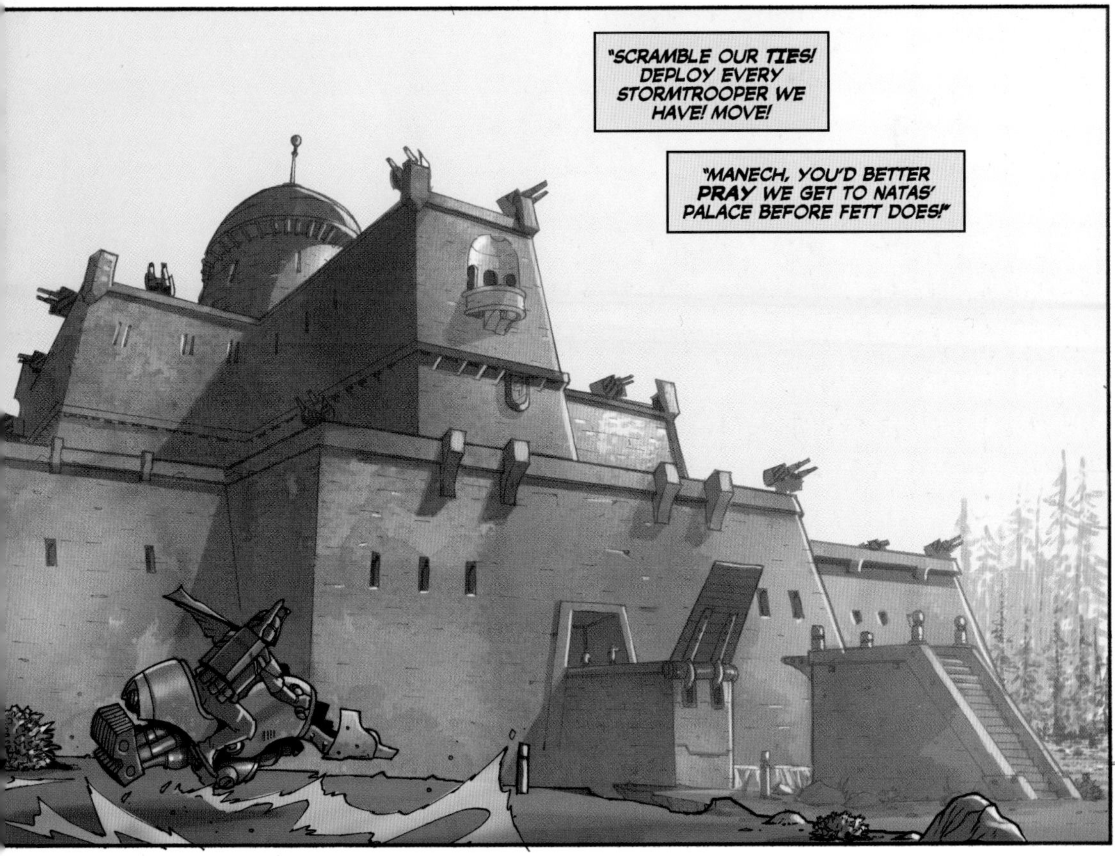
"SCRAMBLE OUR TIES! DEPLOY EVERY STORMTROOPER WE HAVE! MOVE!
"MANECH, YOU'D BETTER PRAY WE GET TO NATAS' PALACE BEFORE FETT DOES!"

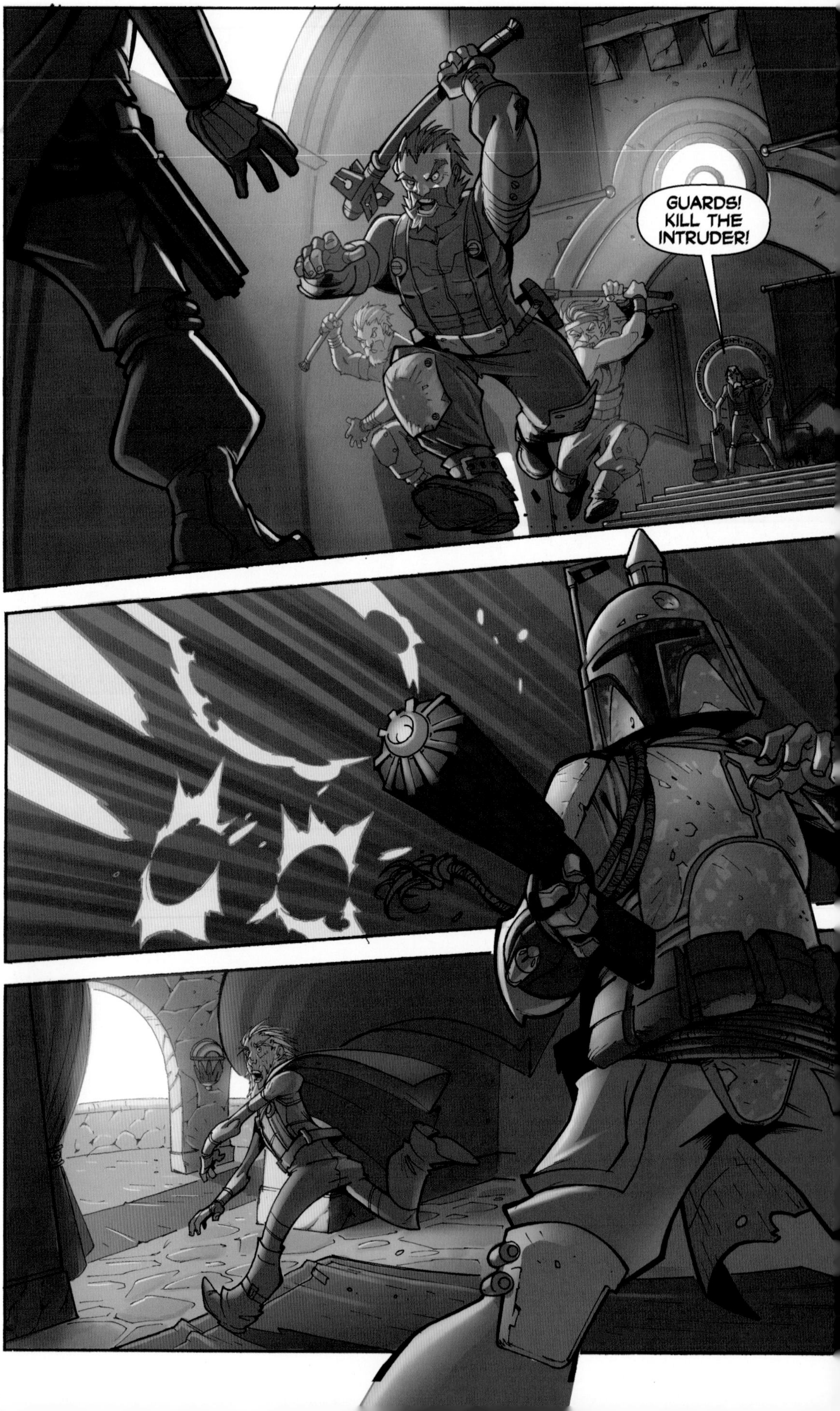
GUARDS! KILL THE INTRUDER!

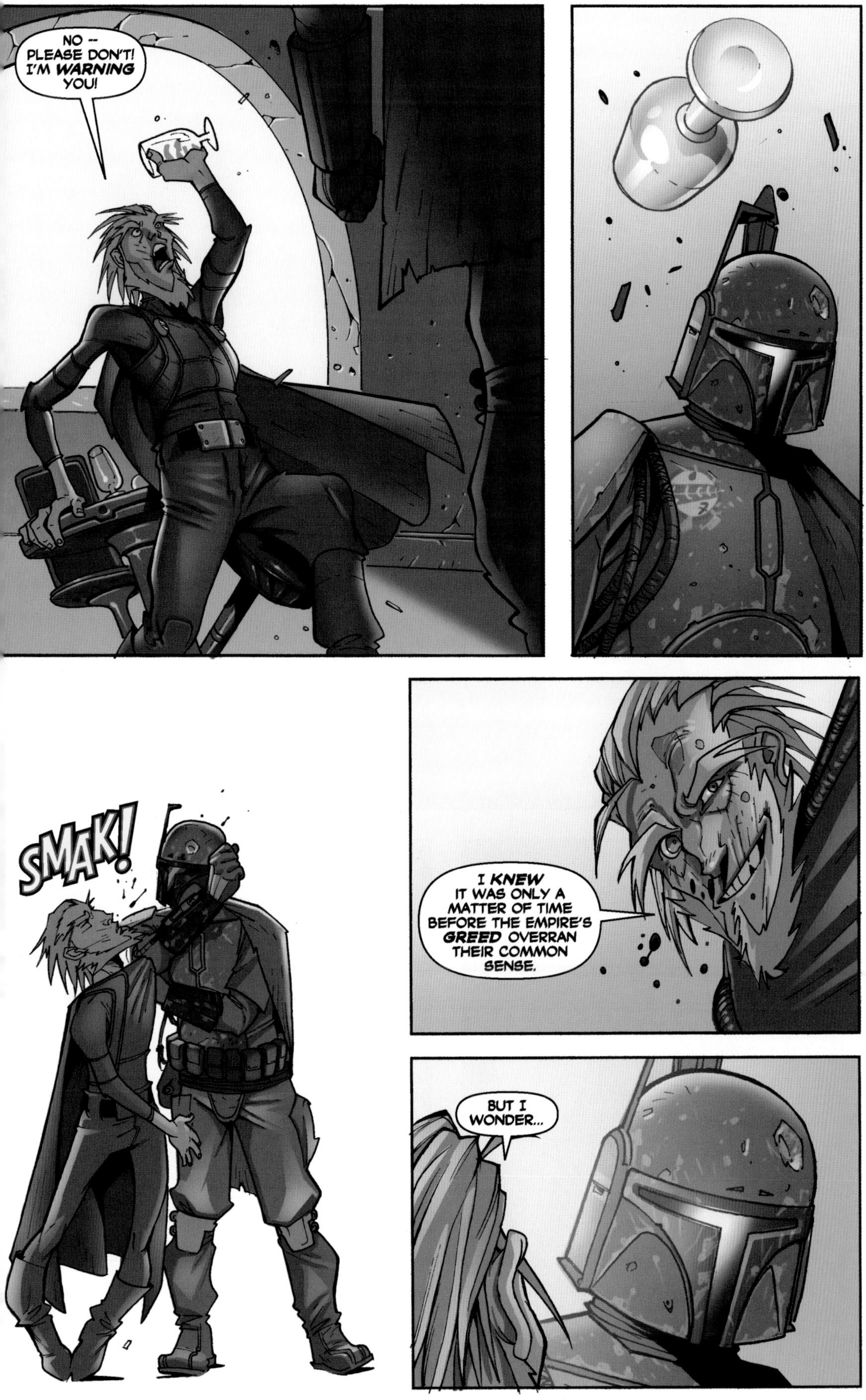
NO -- PLEASE DON'T! I'M WARNING YOU!
SMAK!
I KNEW IT WAS ONLY A MATTER OF TIME BEFORE THE EMPIRE'S GREED OVERRAN THEIR COMMON SENSE.
BUT I WONDER...

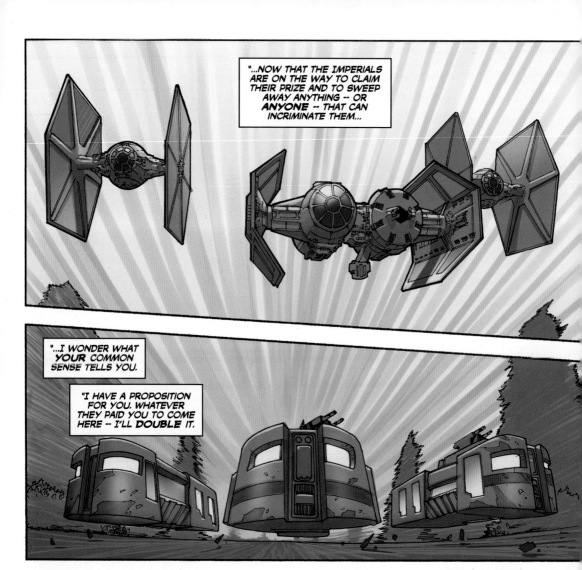

"...NOW THAT THE IMPERIALS ARE ON THE WAY TO CLAIM THEIR PRIZE AND TO SWEEP AWAY ANYTHING -- OR **ANYONE** -- THAT CAN INCRIMINATE THEM...

"...I WONDER WHAT **YOUR** COMMON SENSE TELLS YOU.

"I HAVE A PROPOSITION FOR YOU. WHATEVER THEY PAID YOU TO COME HERE -- I'LL **DOUBLE** IT.

"MAKE THOSE FOOLS SORRY."

THAT'S JUST WHAT I WAS THINKING.

I WANT PAYMENT UP FRONT.

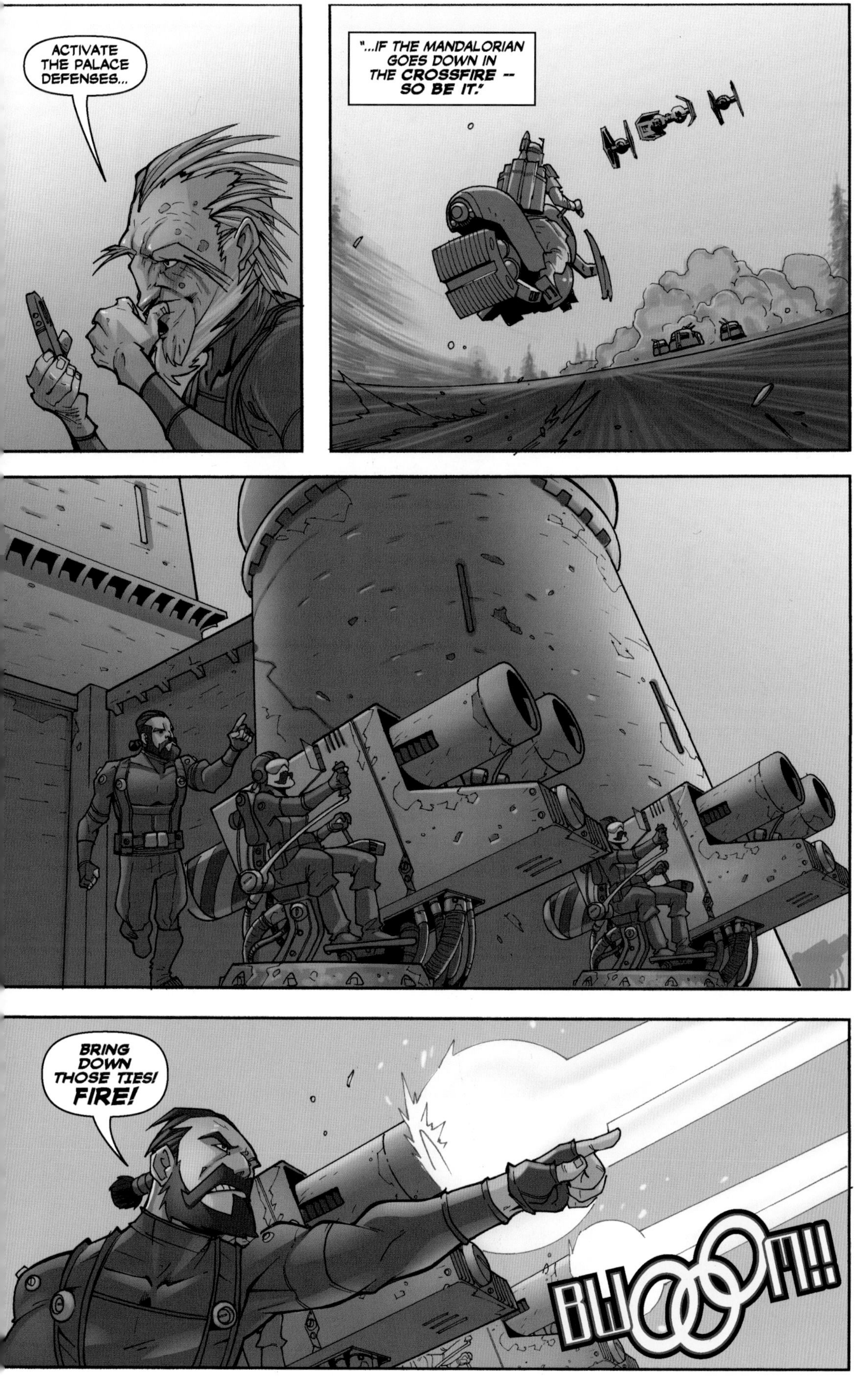
ACTIVATE THE PALACE DEFENSES...
"...IF THE MANDALORIAN GOES DOWN IN THE CROSSFIRE -- SO BE IT."
BRING DOWN THOSE TIES! FIRE!
BWOOOM!!

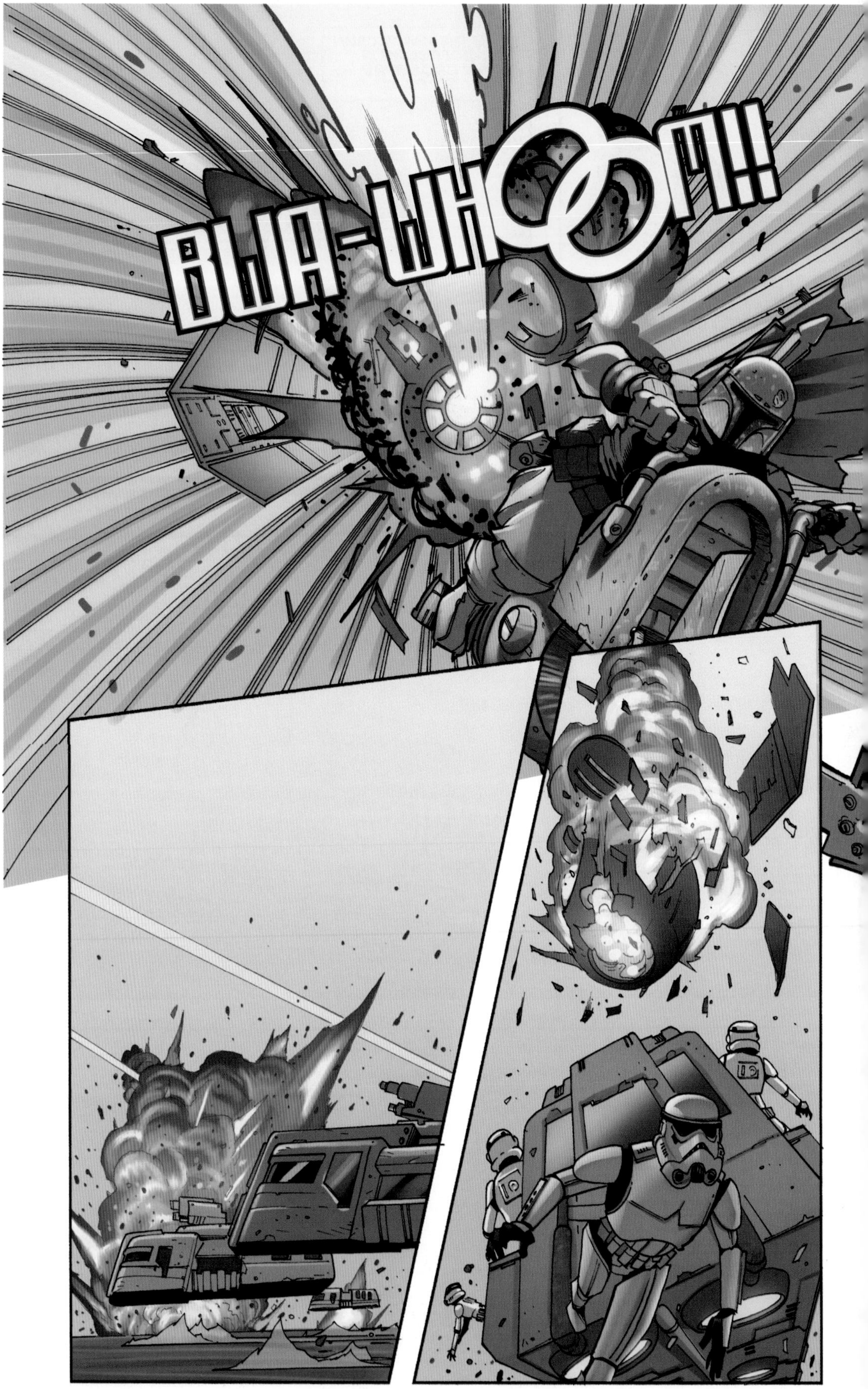
BWA-WHOOM!!

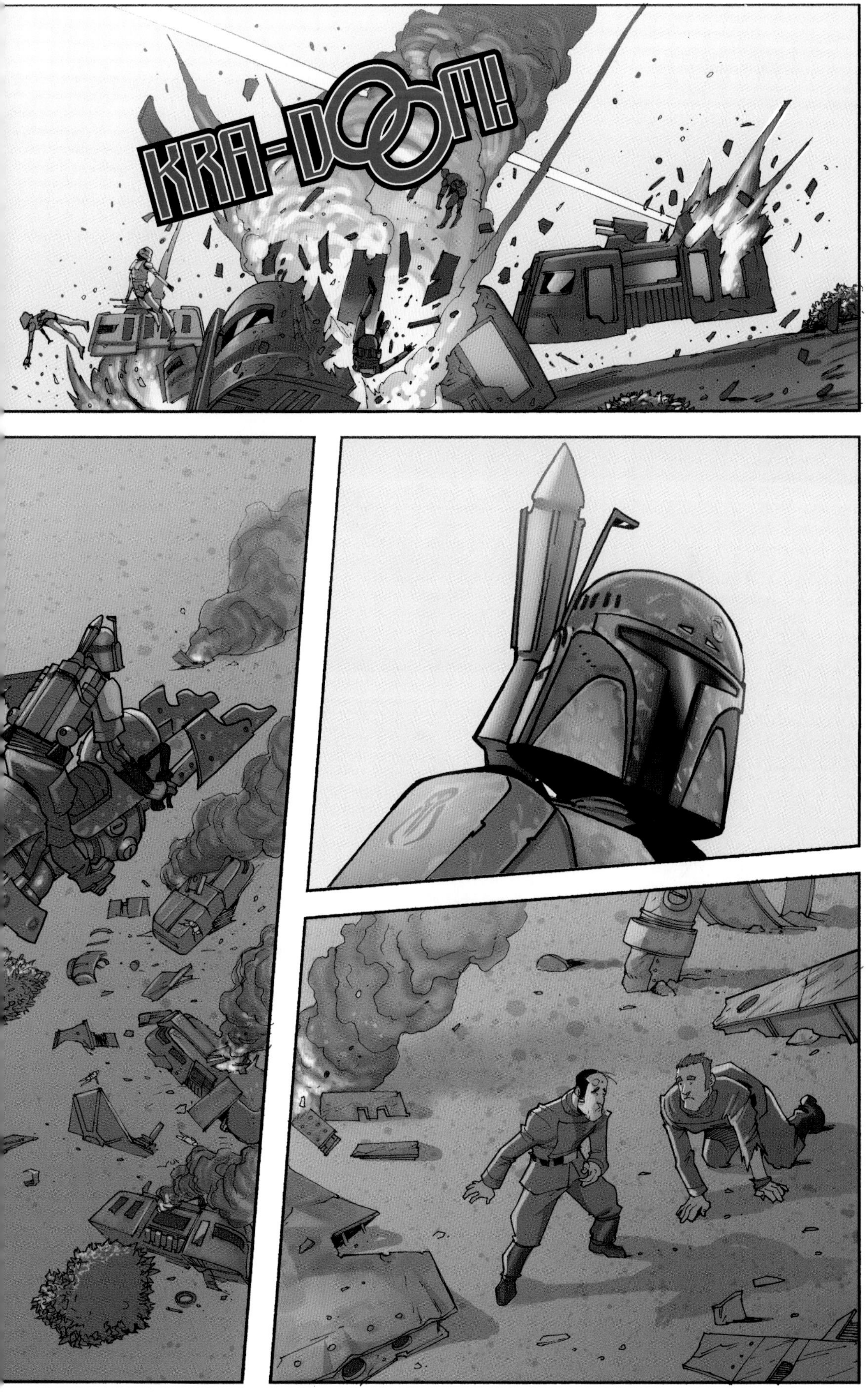
KRA-DOOM!

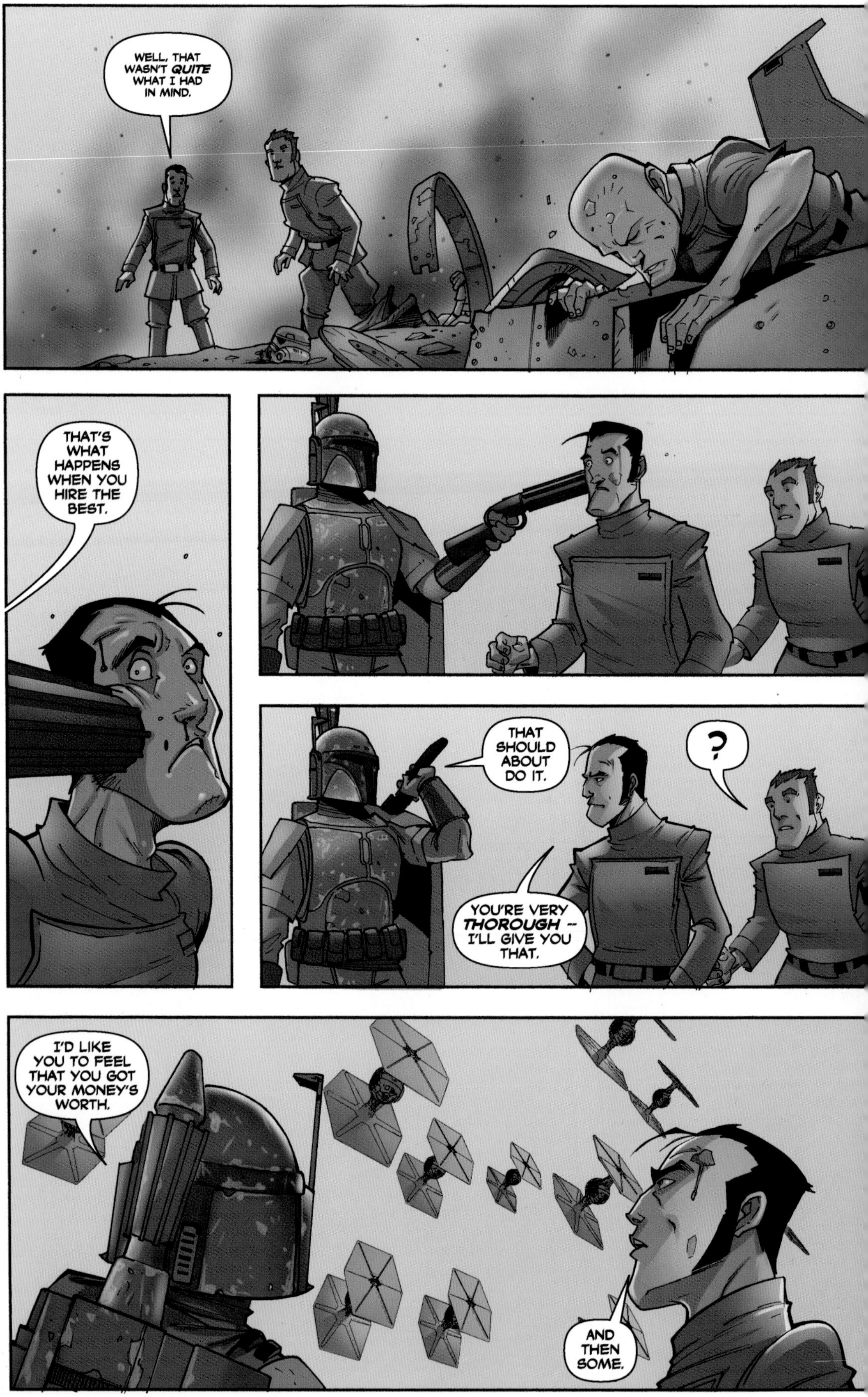

WELL, THAT WASN'T *QUITE* WHAT I HAD IN MIND.
THAT'S WHAT HAPPENS WHEN YOU HIRE THE BEST.
THAT SHOULD ABOUT DO IT.
?
YOU'RE VERY *THOROUGH* -- I'LL GIVE YOU THAT.
I'D LIKE YOU TO FEEL THAT YOU GOT YOUR MONEY'S WORTH.
AND THEN SOME.

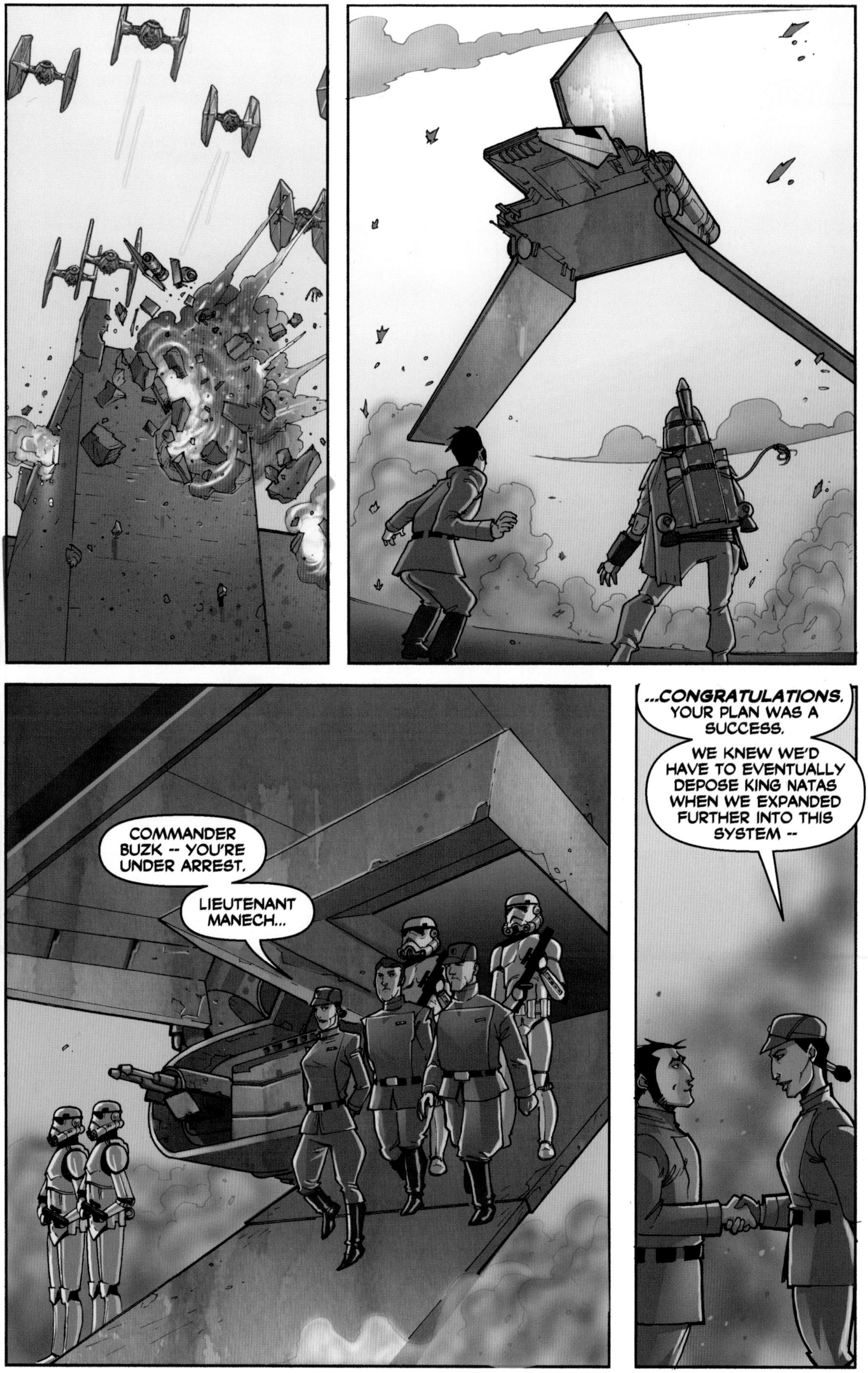
COMMANDER BUZK -- YOU'RE UNDER ARREST.
LIEUTENANT MANECH...
...CONGRATULATIONS. YOUR PLAN WAS A SUCCESS.
WE KNEW WE'D HAVE TO EVENTUALLY DEPOSE KING NATAS WHEN WE EXPANDED FURTHER INTO THIS SYSTEM --

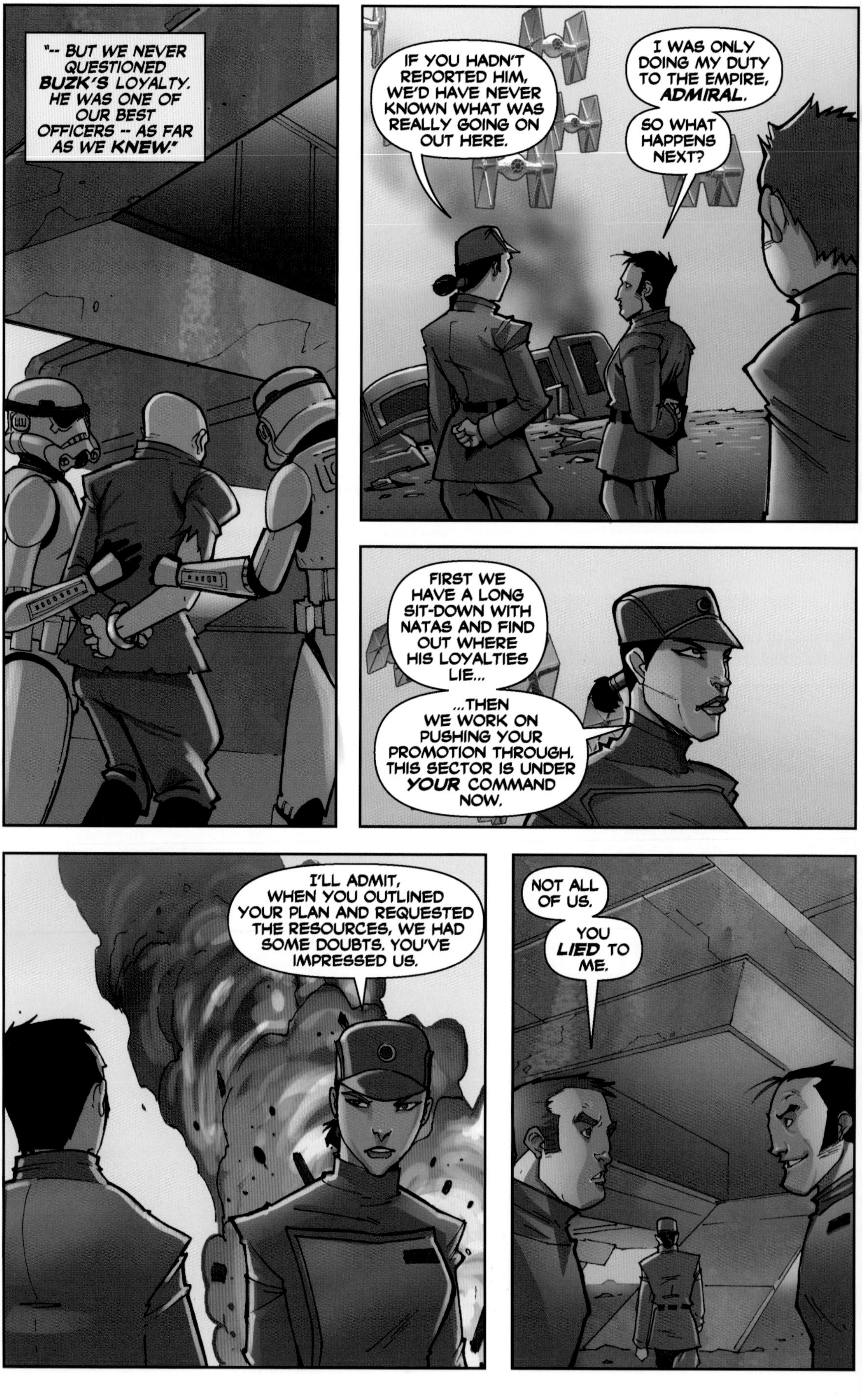
"-- BUT WE NEVER QUESTIONED BUZK'S LOYALTY. HE WAS ONE OF OUR BEST OFFICERS -- AS FAR AS WE KNEW."
IF YOU HADN'T REPORTED HIM, WE'D HAVE NEVER KNOWN WHAT WAS REALLY GOING ON OUT HERE.
I WAS ONLY DOING MY DUTY TO THE EMPIRE, ADMIRAL.
SO WHAT HAPPENS NEXT?
FIRST WE HAVE A LONG SIT-DOWN WITH NATAS AND FIND OUT WHERE HIS LOYALTIES LIE...
...THEN WE WORK ON PUSHING YOUR PROMOTION THROUGH. THIS SECTOR IS UNDER YOUR COMMAND NOW.
I'LL ADMIT, WHEN YOU OUTLINED YOUR PLAN AND REQUESTED THE RESOURCES, WE HAD SOME DOUBTS. YOU'VE IMPRESSED US.
NOT ALL OF US.
YOU LIED TO ME.

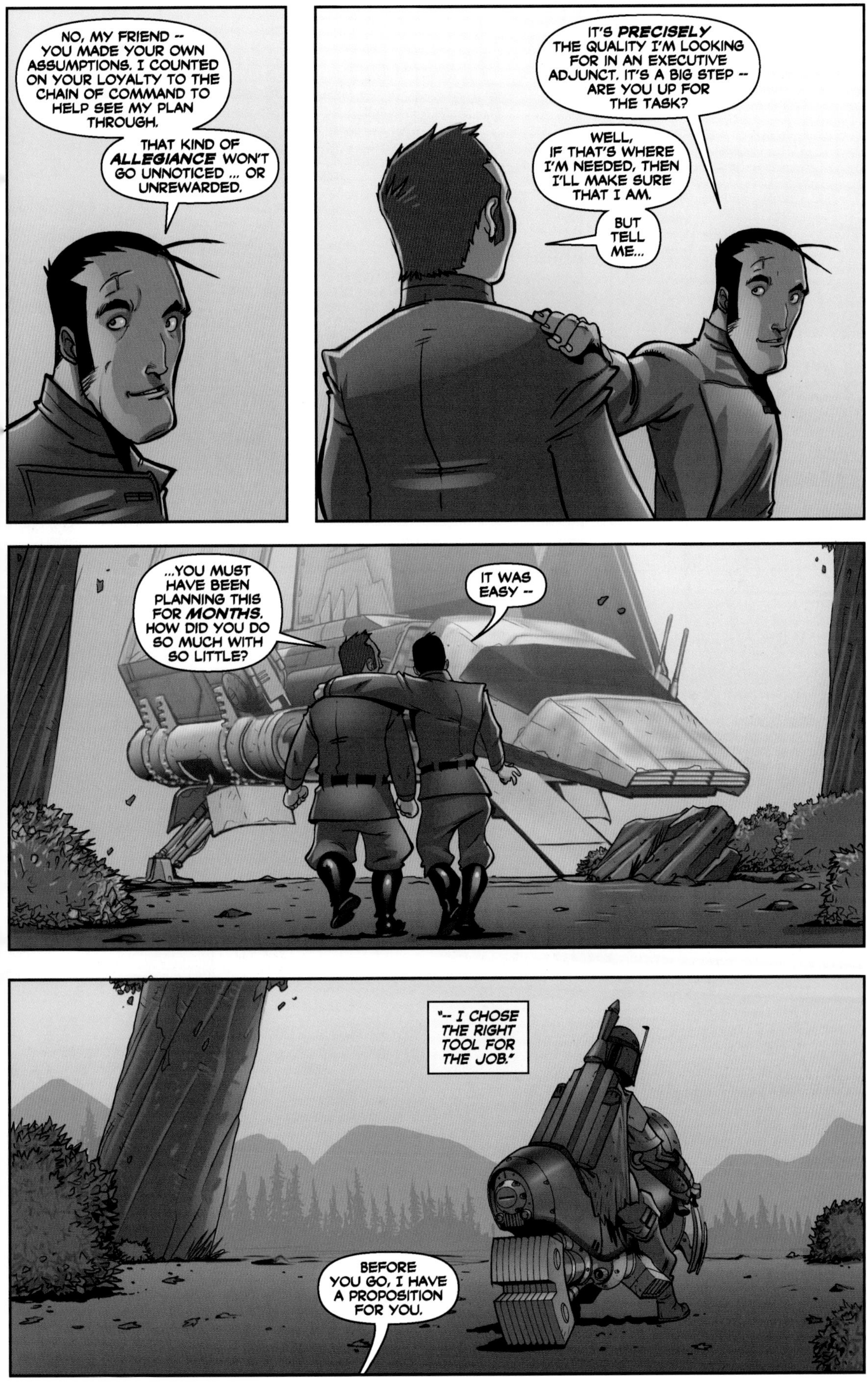
NO, MY FRIEND -- YOU MADE YOUR OWN ASSUMPTIONS. I COUNTED ON YOUR LOYALTY TO THE CHAIN OF COMMAND TO HELP SEE MY PLAN THROUGH.
THAT KIND OF ALLEGIANCE WON'T GO UNNOTICED ... OR UNREWARDED.
IT'S PRECISELY THE QUALITY I'M LOOKING FOR IN AN EXECUTIVE ADJUNCT. IT'S A BIG STEP -- ARE YOU UP FOR THE TASK?
WELL, IF THAT'S WHERE I'M NEEDED, THEN I'LL MAKE SURE THAT I AM.
BUT TELL ME...
...YOU MUST HAVE BEEN PLANNING THIS FOR MONTHS. HOW DID YOU DO SO MUCH WITH SO LITTLE?
IT WAS EASY --
"-- I CHOSE THE RIGHT TOOL FOR THE JOB."
BEFORE YOU GO, I HAVE A PROPOSITION FOR YOU.

THIS IS WILD COUNTRY OUT HERE. YOU INTERESTED IN HELPING THE EMPIRE TAME IT?

YOU COULDN'T AFFORD ME ON A FULL-TIME BASIS.

TELL ME SOMETHING -- YOU COULD'VE LET THINGS STAND OUT HERE, TAKEN OVER THE OPERATION AND MADE YOURSELF A RICH MAN.

WHY BREAK IT UP?

I'M THINKING *BIGGER*. IT'S ONLY A MATTER OF TIME BEFORE THE EMPIRE'S REACH EXTENDS TO THIS SECTOR. WHEN THAT HAPPENS, *POWER* WILL BE MORE IMPORTANT THAN WEALTH.

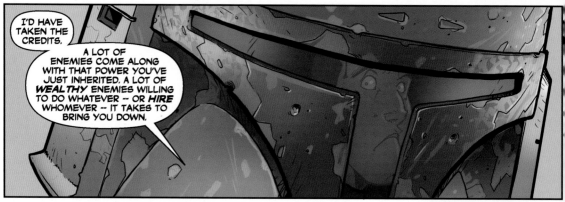

I'D HAVE TAKEN THE CREDITS.

A LOT OF ENEMIES COME ALONG WITH THAT POWER YOU'VE JUST INHERITED. A LOT OF *WEALTHY* ENEMIES WILLING TO DO WHATEVER -- OR *HIRE* WHOMEVER -- IT TAKES TO BRING YOU DOWN.

VRROOOMM!!

SEE YOU AROUND.

THE END

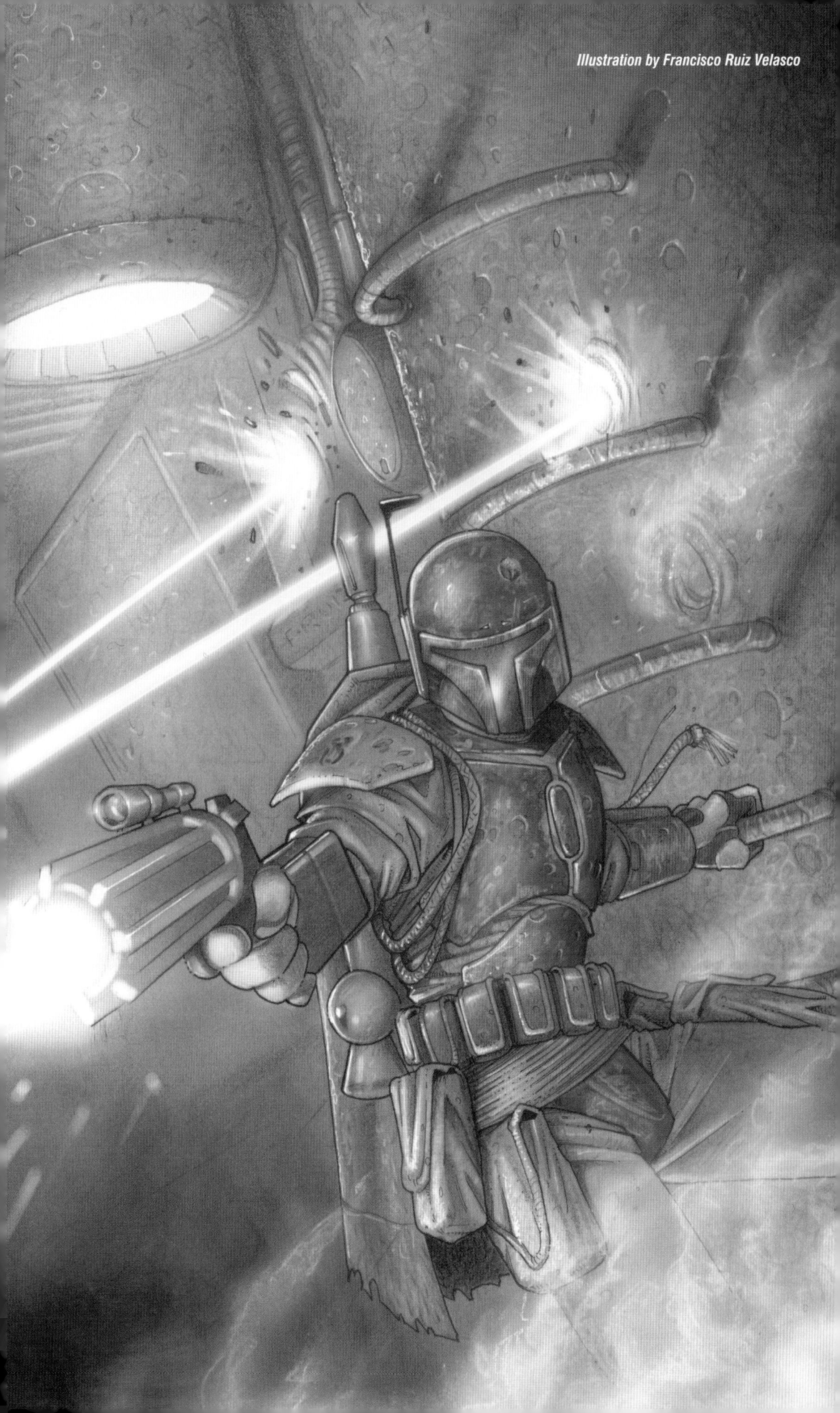
Illustration by Francisco Ruiz Velasco

AGENT OF DOOM

SCRIPT
John Ostrander

ART
Cam Kennedy

COLORS
Chris Blythe

LETTERS
Steve Dutro

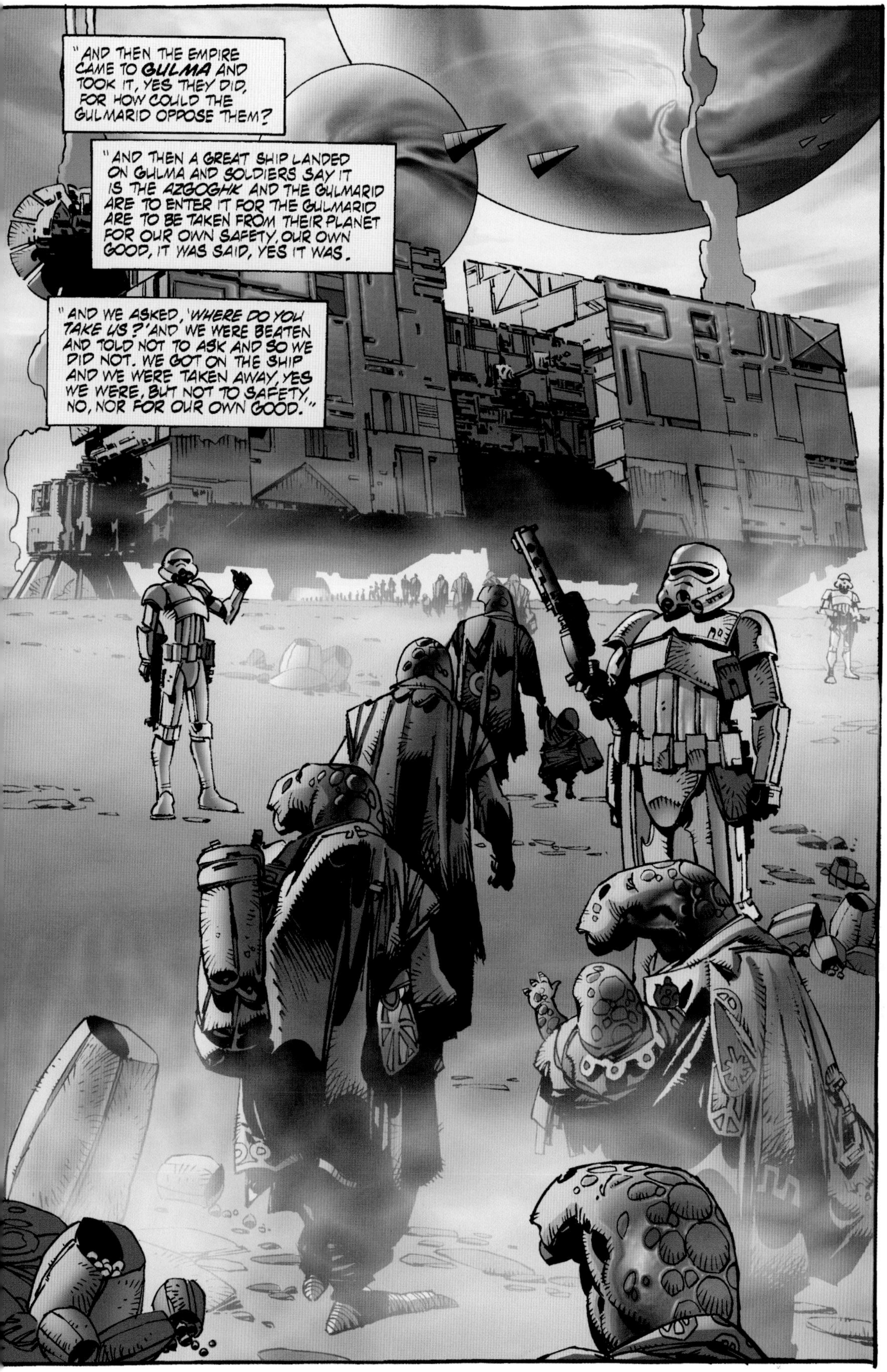
"AND THEN THE EMPIRE CAME TO GULMA AND TOOK IT, YES THEY DID, FOR HOW COULD THE GULMARID OPPOSE THEM?
"AND THEN A GREAT SHIP LANDED ON GULMA AND SOLDIERS SAY IT IS THE AZGOGHK AND THE GULMARID ARE TO ENTER IT FOR THE GULMARID ARE TO BE TAKEN FROM THEIR PLANET FOR OUR OWN SAFETY, OUR OWN GOOD, IT WAS SAID, YES IT WAS.
"AND WE ASKED, 'WHERE DO YOU TAKE US?' AND WE WERE BEATEN AND TOLD NOT TO ASK AND SO WE DID NOT. WE GOT ON THE SHIP AND WE WERE TAKEN AWAY, YES WE WERE, BUT NOT TO SAFETY, NO, NOR FOR OUR OWN GOOD."

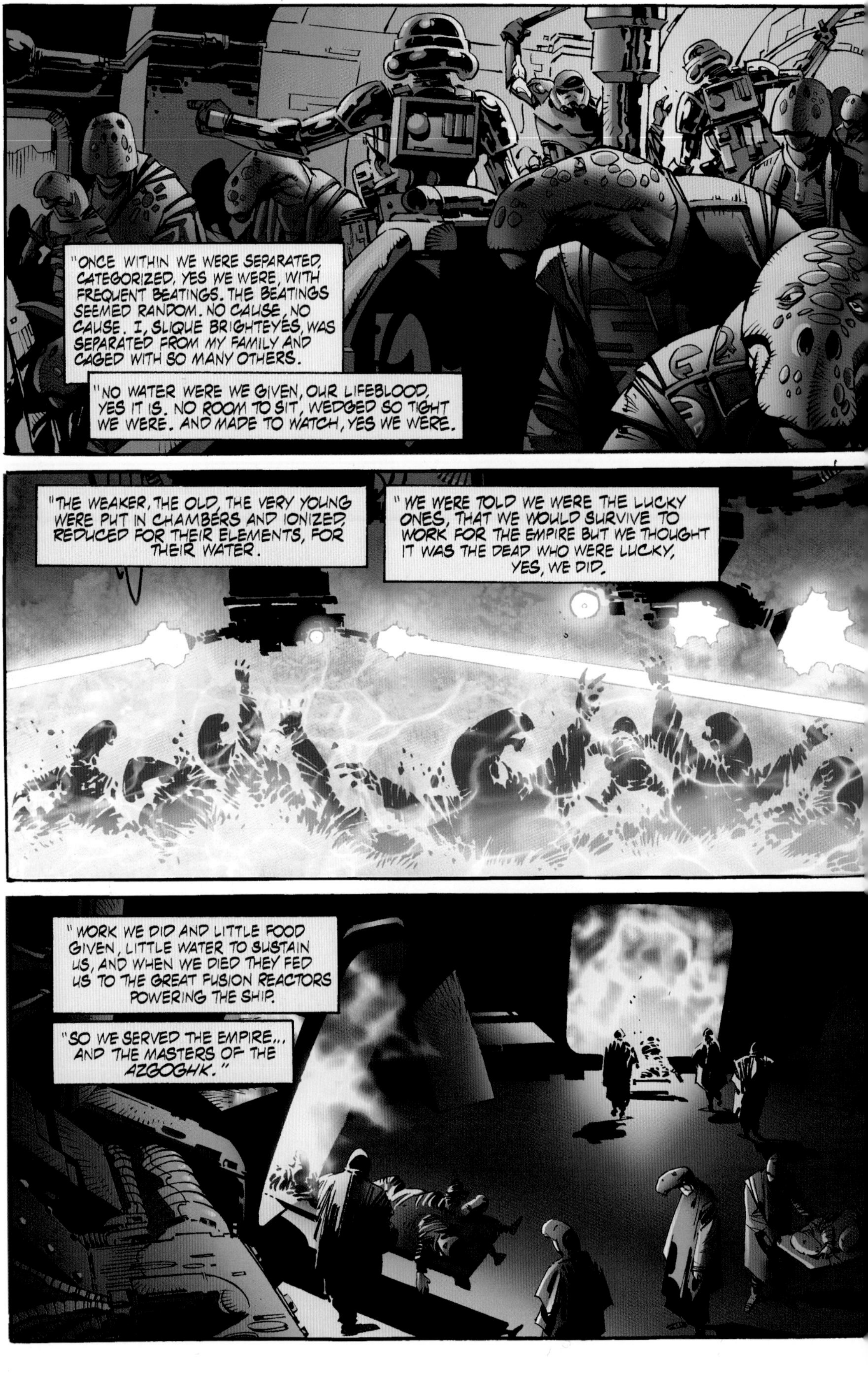
"ONCE WITHIN WE WERE SEPARATED, CATEGORIZED, YES WE WERE, WITH FREQUENT BEATINGS. THE BEATINGS SEEMED RANDOM. NO CAUSE, NO CAUSE. I, SLIQUE BRIGHTEYES, WAS SEPARATED FROM MY FAMILY AND CAGED WITH SO MANY OTHERS.
"NO WATER WERE WE GIVEN, OUR LIFEBLOOD, YES IT IS. NO ROOM TO SIT, WEDGED SO TIGHT WE WERE. AND MADE TO WATCH, YES WE WERE.
"THE WEAKER, THE OLD, THE VERY YOUNG WERE PUT IN CHAMBERS AND IONIZED, REDUCED FOR THEIR ELEMENTS, FOR THEIR WATER.
"WE WERE TOLD WE WERE THE LUCKY ONES, THAT WE WOULD SURVIVE TO WORK FOR THE EMPIRE BUT WE THOUGHT IT WAS THE DEAD WHO WERE LUCKY, YES, WE DID.
"WORK WE DID AND LITTLE FOOD GIVEN, LITTLE WATER TO SUSTAIN US, AND WHEN WE DIED THEY FED US TO THE GREAT FUSION REACTORS POWERING THE SHIP.
"SO WE SERVED THE EMPIRE... AND THE MASTERS OF THE *AZGOGHK*."

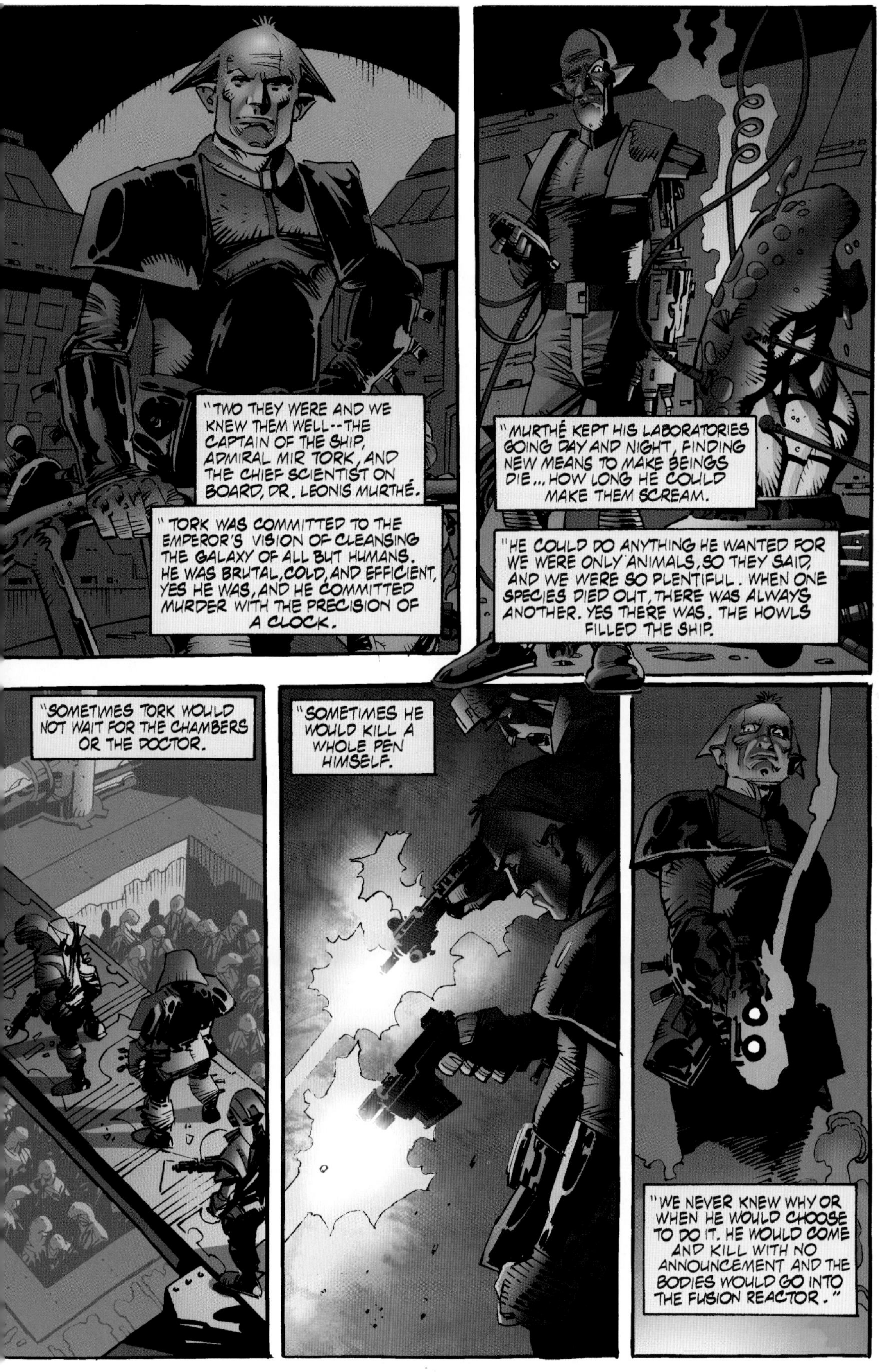
"TWO THEY WERE AND WE KNEW THEM WELL--THE CAPTAIN OF THE SHIP, ADMIRAL MIR TORK, AND THE CHIEF SCIENTIST ON BOARD, DR. LEONIS MURTHÉ.
"TORK WAS COMMITTED TO THE EMPEROR'S VISION OF CLEANSING THE GALAXY OF ALL BUT HUMANS. HE WAS BRUTAL, COLD, AND EFFICIENT, YES HE WAS, AND HE COMMITTED MURDER WITH THE PRECISION OF A CLOCK.
"MURTHÉ KEPT HIS LABORATORIES GOING DAY AND NIGHT, FINDING NEW MEANS TO MAKE BEINGS DIE... HOW LONG HE COULD MAKE THEM SCREAM.
"HE COULD DO ANYTHING HE WANTED FOR WE WERE ONLY ANIMALS, SO THEY SAID, AND WE WERE SO PLENTIFUL. WHEN ONE SPECIES DIED OUT, THERE WAS ALWAYS ANOTHER. YES THERE WAS. THE HOWLS FILLED THE SHIP.
"SOMETIMES TORK WOULD NOT WAIT FOR THE CHAMBERS OR THE DOCTOR.
"SOMETIMES HE WOULD KILL A WHOLE PEN HIMSELF.
"WE NEVER KNEW WHY OR WHEN HE WOULD CHOOSE TO DO IT. HE WOULD COME AND KILL WITH NO ANNOUNCEMENT AND THE BODIES WOULD GO INTO THE FUSION REACTOR."

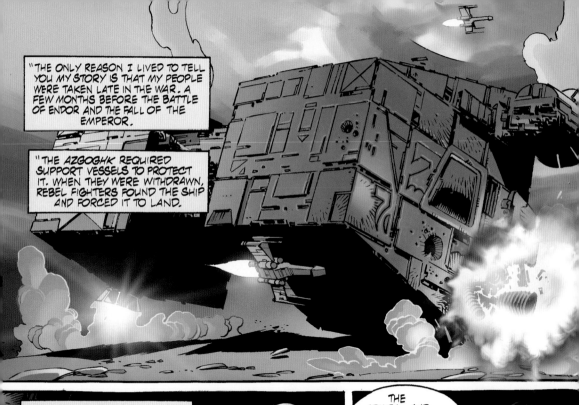

"THE ONLY REASON I LIVED TO TELL YOU MY STORY IS THAT MY PEOPLE WERE TAKEN LATE IN THE WAR. A FEW MONTHS BEFORE THE BATTLE OF ENDOR AND THE FALL OF THE EMPEROR.

"THE AZGOGHK REQUIRED SUPPORT VESSELS TO PROTECT IT. WHEN THEY WERE WITHDRAWN, REBEL FIGHTERS FOUND THE SHIP AND FORCED IT TO LAND.

"WE WERE SAVED, YES WE WERE, BUT OUR SAVIORS COULD NOT HIDE HOW APPALLED THEY WERE BY WHAT THEY FOUND.

"SO SICK WERE WE THAT FEW WHO SURVIVED THE AZGOGHK LASTED LONG AFTER FREEDOM. MANY CHOSE TO LAY DOWN AND DIE, SO TERRIBLE WAS THEIR SUFFERING. SO TERRIBLE."

THE ADMIRAL AND THE DOCTOR ESCAPED, YES THEY DID. THE AZGOGHK WAS LEFT BEHIND, ABANDONED. WE WERE TAKEN TO GULMA, BUT IT HAD BEEN STRIPPED.

WE ARE HOMELESS, YES, AND DYING ALSO. AND THE ADMIRAL AND THE DOCTOR STILL LIVE AND SO, AT THE LAST, WE COME TO YOU.

WHAT DO YOU WANT FROM ME?

JUSTICE.

IT IS NOT RIGHT. IT IS NOT FAIR, THAT THE LAST OF THE GULMARID DIE BEFORE TORK AND MURTHÉ. WHAT WE WANT, WHAT IS RIGHT, IS THEM DEAD! YES IT IS!

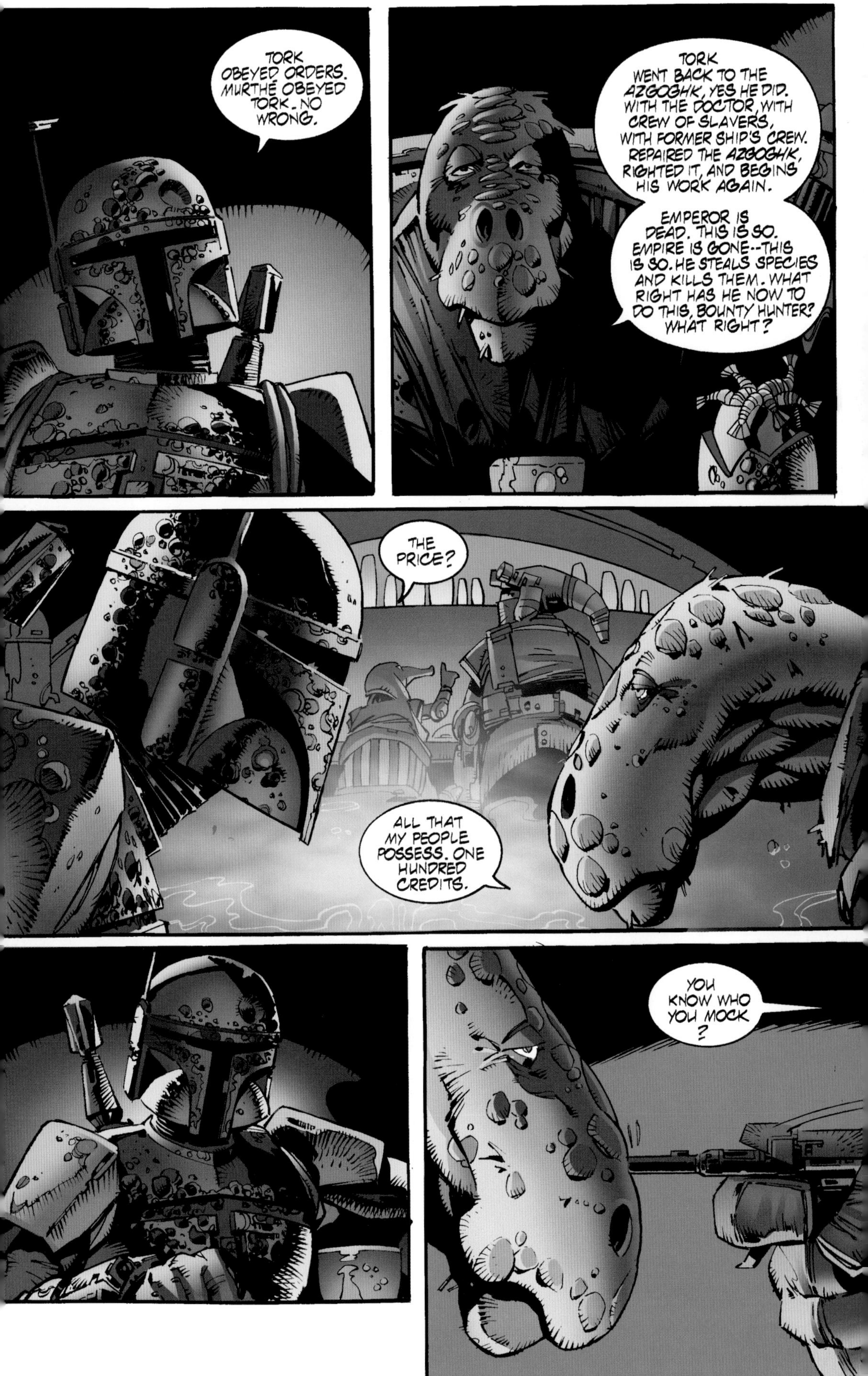
TORK OBEYED ORDERS. MURTHÉ OBEYED TORK. NO WRONG.
TORK WENT BACK TO THE AZGOGHK, YES HE DID. WITH THE DOCTOR, WITH CREW OF SLAVERS, WITH FORMER SHIP'S CREW. REPAIRED THE AZGOGHK, RIGHTED IT, AND BEGINS HIS WORK AGAIN.
EMPEROR IS DEAD. THIS IS SO. EMPIRE IS GONE--THIS IS SO. HE STEALS SPECIES AND KILLS THEM. WHAT RIGHT HAS HE NOW TO DO THIS, BOUNTY HUNTER? WHAT RIGHT?
THE PRICE?
ALL THAT MY PEOPLE POSSESS. ONE HUNDRED CREDITS.
YOU KNOW WHO YOU MOCK?

KNOW THAT YOU WERE BOBA FETT. ONCE, THAT WAS A NAME TO CONJURE FEAR, YES IT WAS.

THAT WAS BEFORE THE JEDI FED YOU TO THE SARLACC.

THAT WAS BEFORE HAN SOLO ESCAPES YOU SO MANY TIMES. SOME NOW ASK--IS IT THE SAME MAN BENEATH THE HELMET?

MANY SPECIES PUT CONTRACT OUT ON TORK AND MURTHÉ. NO ONE WILL TOUCH IT. IMPOSSIBLE, THEY SAY, BUT FETT COULD DO IT. YES, HE COULD.

IF YOU DO THIS, IT WILL NOT BE BECAUSE OF THE MONEY. IT WILL BE SO THAT ALL KNOW WHO IS BOBA FETT. YES.

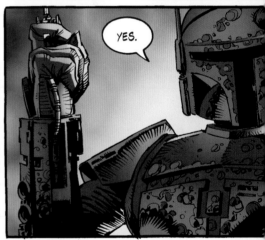

YES.

" WE WILL PROVIDE THE LOCATION OF THE SHIP. WE WILL PROVIDE SPECIFICATIONS GLEANED FROM OLD IMPERIAL FILES. YES WE WILL.

"YOU WILL PROVIDE US WITH THE HEADS OF MURTHÉ AND TORK-- IF YOU ARE BOBA FETT. "

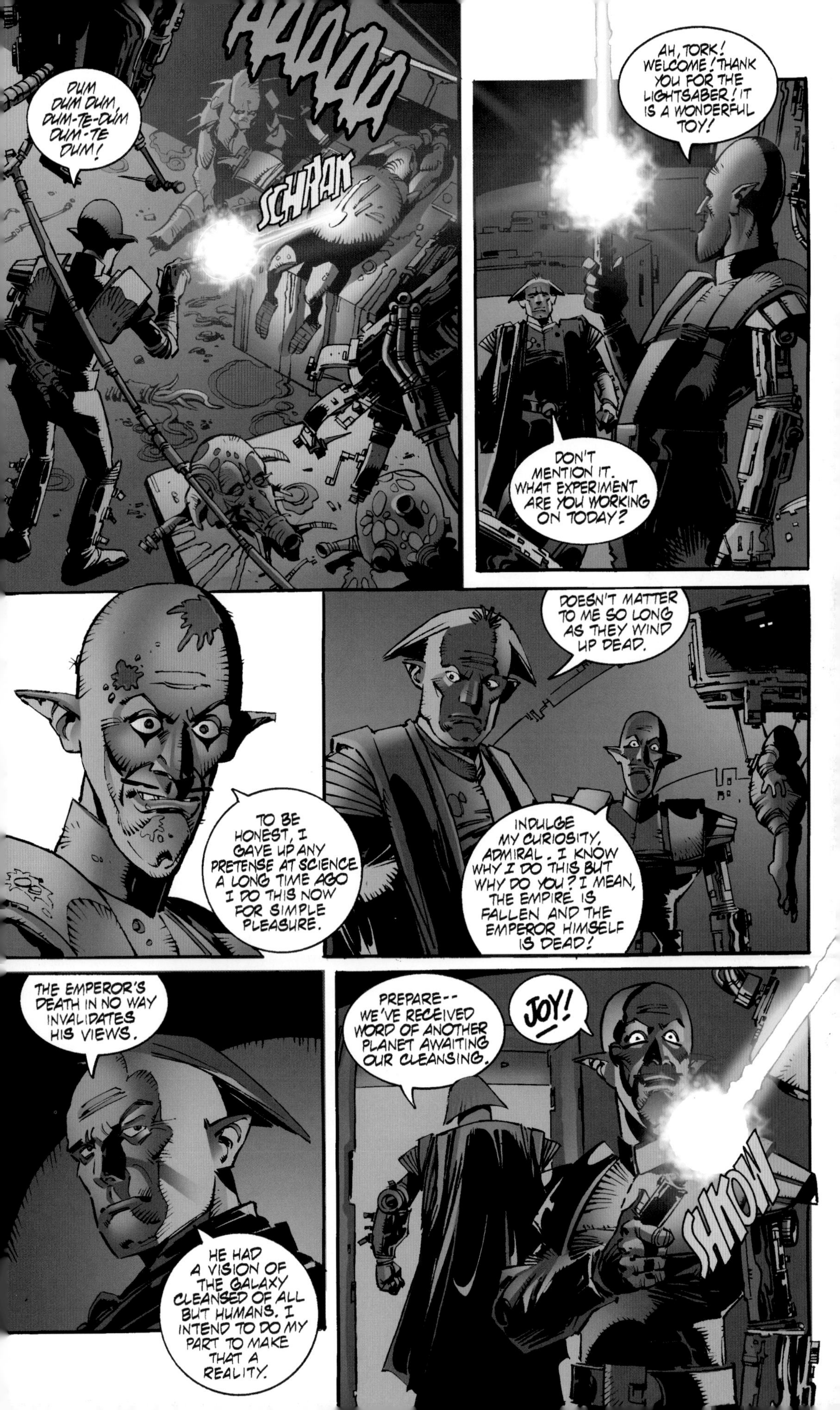
HAAAA
DUM DUM DUM, DUM-TE-DUM DUM-TE DUM!
SCHRAK
AH, TORK! WELCOME! THANK YOU FOR THE LIGHTSABER! IT IS A WONDERFUL TOY!
DON'T MENTION IT. WHAT EXPERIMENT ARE YOU WORKING ON TODAY?
TO BE HONEST, I GAVE UP ANY PRETENSE AT SCIENCE A LONG TIME AGO. I DO THIS NOW FOR SIMPLE PLEASURE.
DOESN'T MATTER TO ME SO LONG AS THEY WIND UP DEAD.
INDULGE MY CURIOSITY, ADMIRAL. I KNOW WHY I DO THIS BUT WHY DO YOU? I MEAN, THE EMPIRE IS FALLEN AND THE EMPEROR HIMSELF IS DEAD!
THE EMPEROR'S DEATH IN NO WAY INVALIDATES HIS VIEWS.
HE HAD A VISION OF THE GALAXY CLEANSED OF ALL BUT HUMANS. I INTEND TO DO MY PART TO MAKE THAT A REALITY.
PREPARE-- WE'VE RECEIVED WORD OF ANOTHER PLANET AWAITING OUR CLEANSING.
JOY!
SHOOM

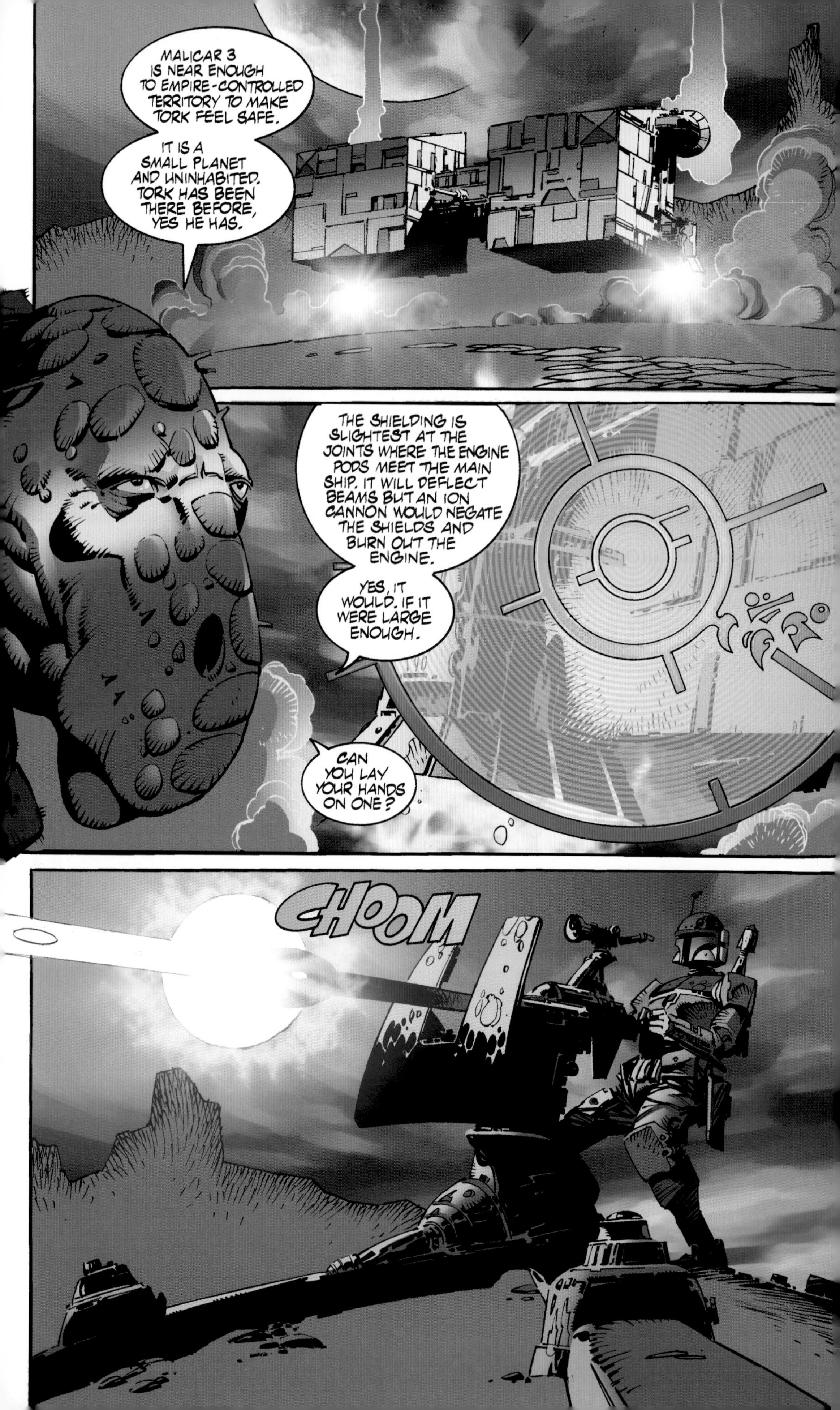
MALICAR 3 IS NEAR ENOUGH TO EMPIRE-CONTROLLED TERRITORY TO MAKE TORK FEEL SAFE.
IT IS A SMALL PLANET AND UNINHABITED. TORK HAS BEEN THERE BEFORE, YES HE HAS.
THE SHIELDING IS SLIGHTEST AT THE JOINTS WHERE THE ENGINE PODS MEET THE MAIN SHIP. IT WILL DEFLECT BEAMS BUT AN ION CANNON WOULD NEGATE THE SHIELDS AND BURN OUT THE ENGINE.
YES, IT WOULD. IF IT WERE LARGE ENOUGH.
CAN YOU LAY YOUR HANDS ON ONE?
CHOOM

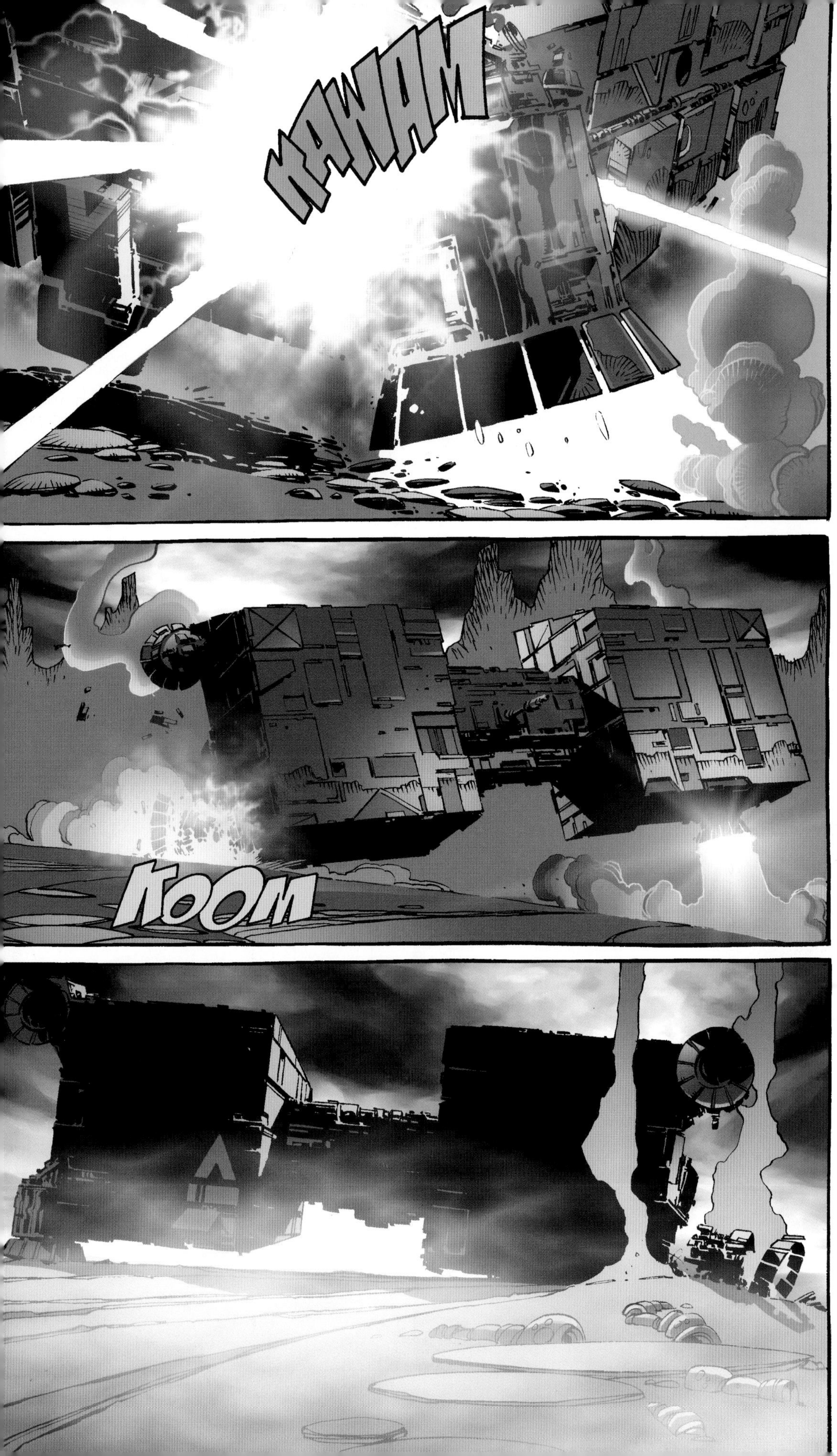
KAWAM
KOOM

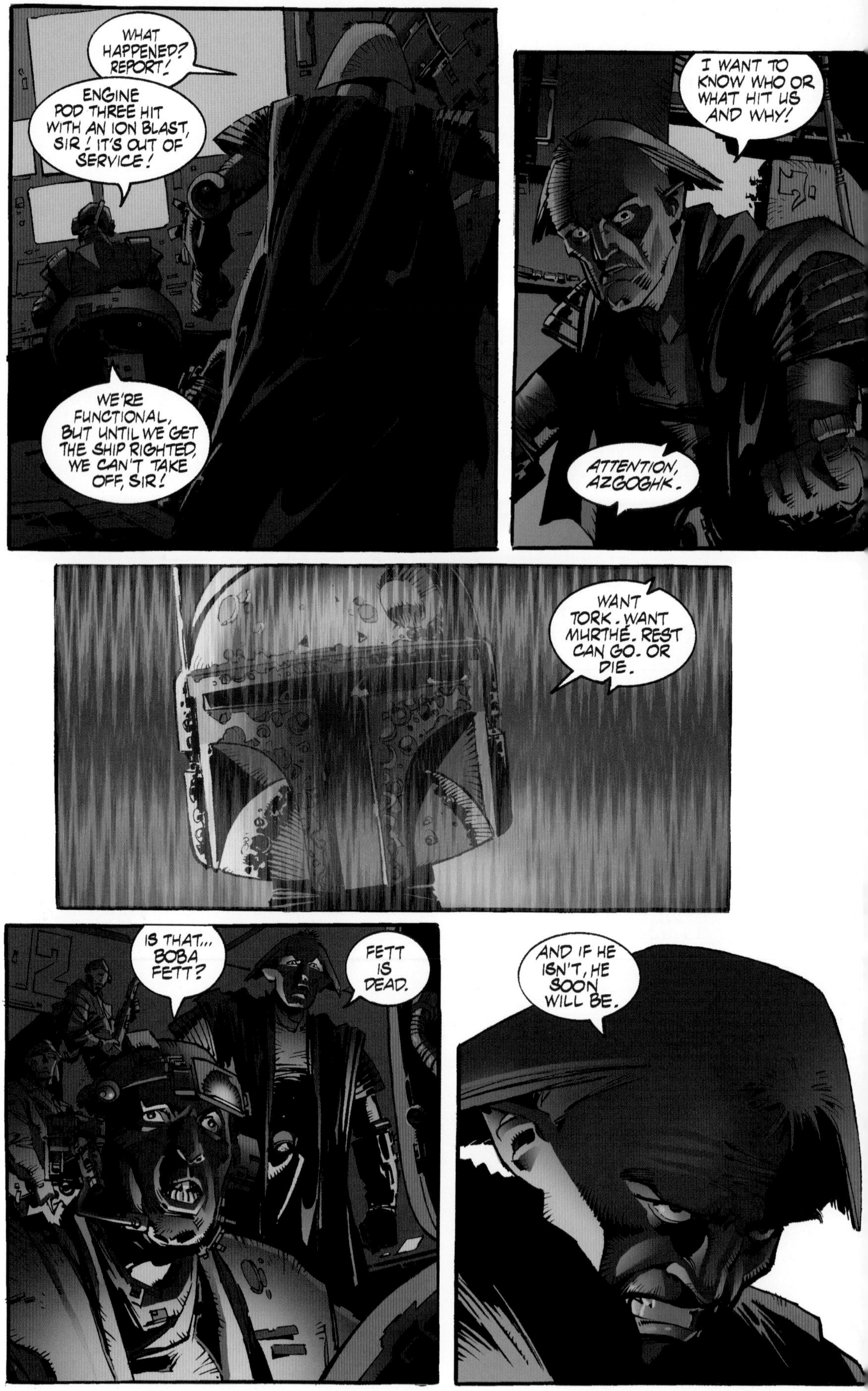

WHAT HAPPENED? REPORT!
ENGINE POD THREE HIT WITH AN ION BLAST, SIR! IT'S OUT OF SERVICE!
WE'RE FUNCTIONAL, BUT UNTIL WE GET THE SHIP RIGHTED, WE CAN'T TAKE OFF, SIR!
I WANT TO KNOW WHO OR WHAT HIT US AND WHY!
ATTENTION, AZGOGHK.
WANT TORK. WANT MURTHÉ. REST CAN GO. OR DIE.
IS THAT... BOBA FETT?
FETT IS DEAD.
AND IF HE ISN'T, HE SOON WILL BE.

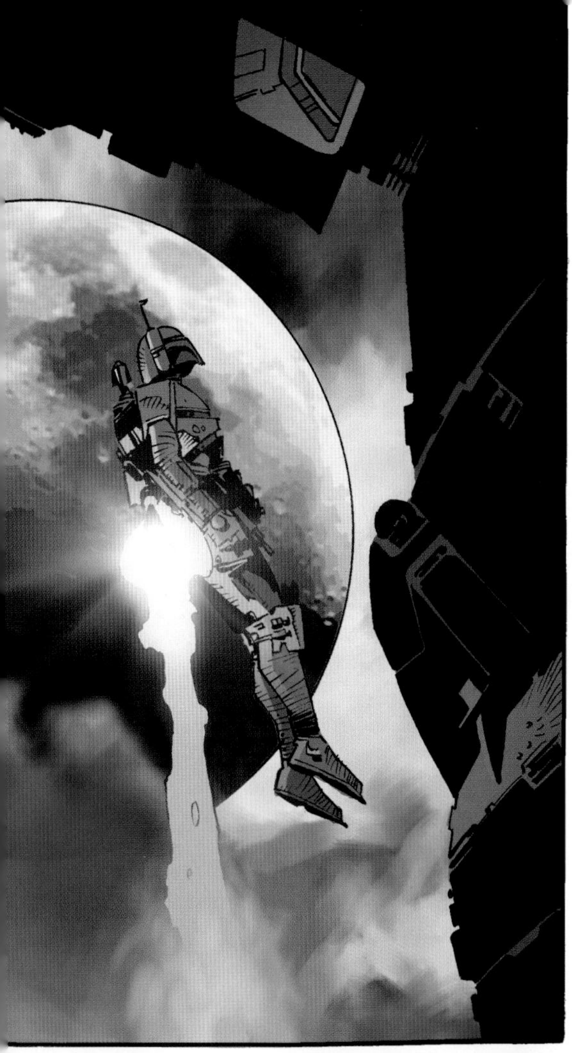

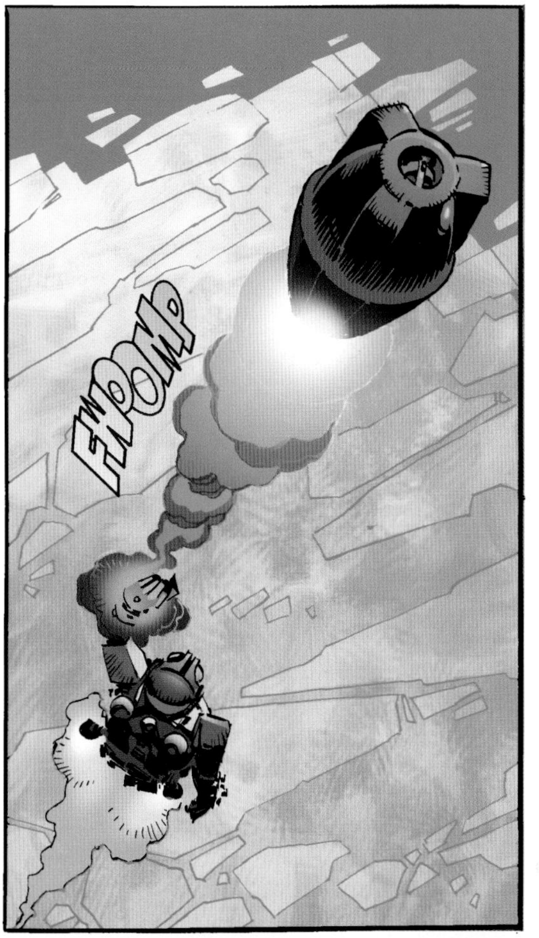

FWOOMP

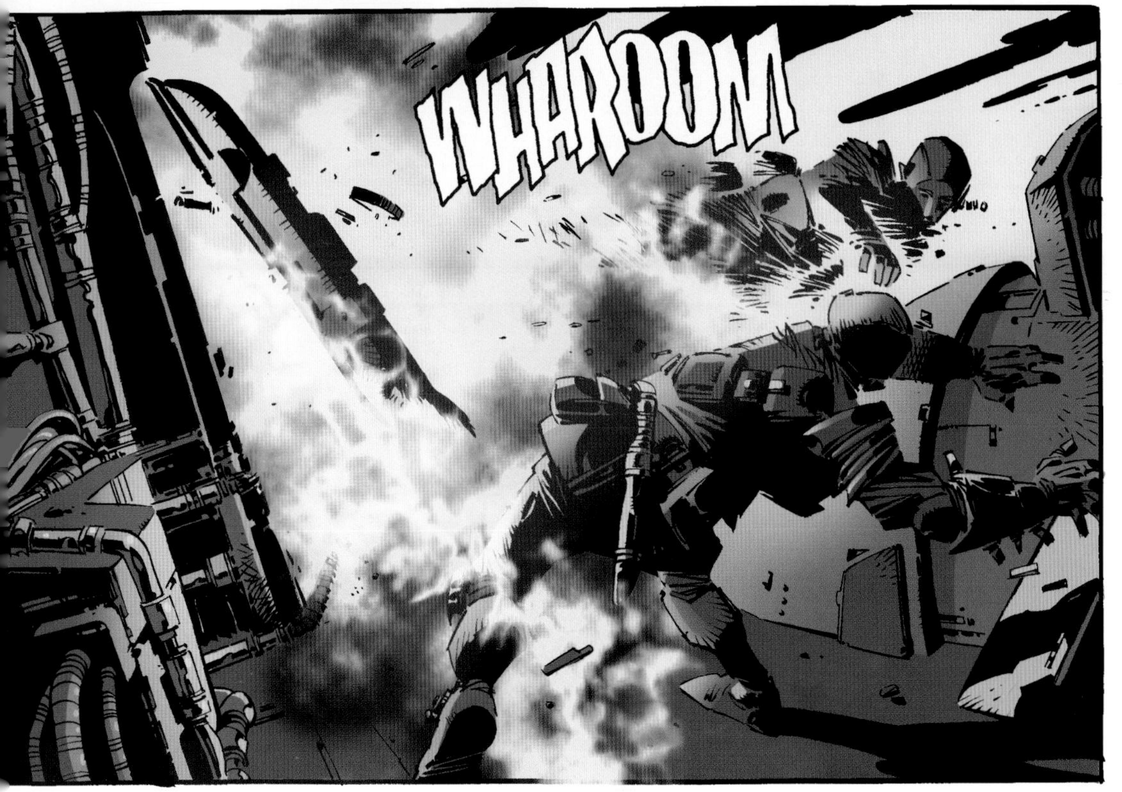

WHAROOM

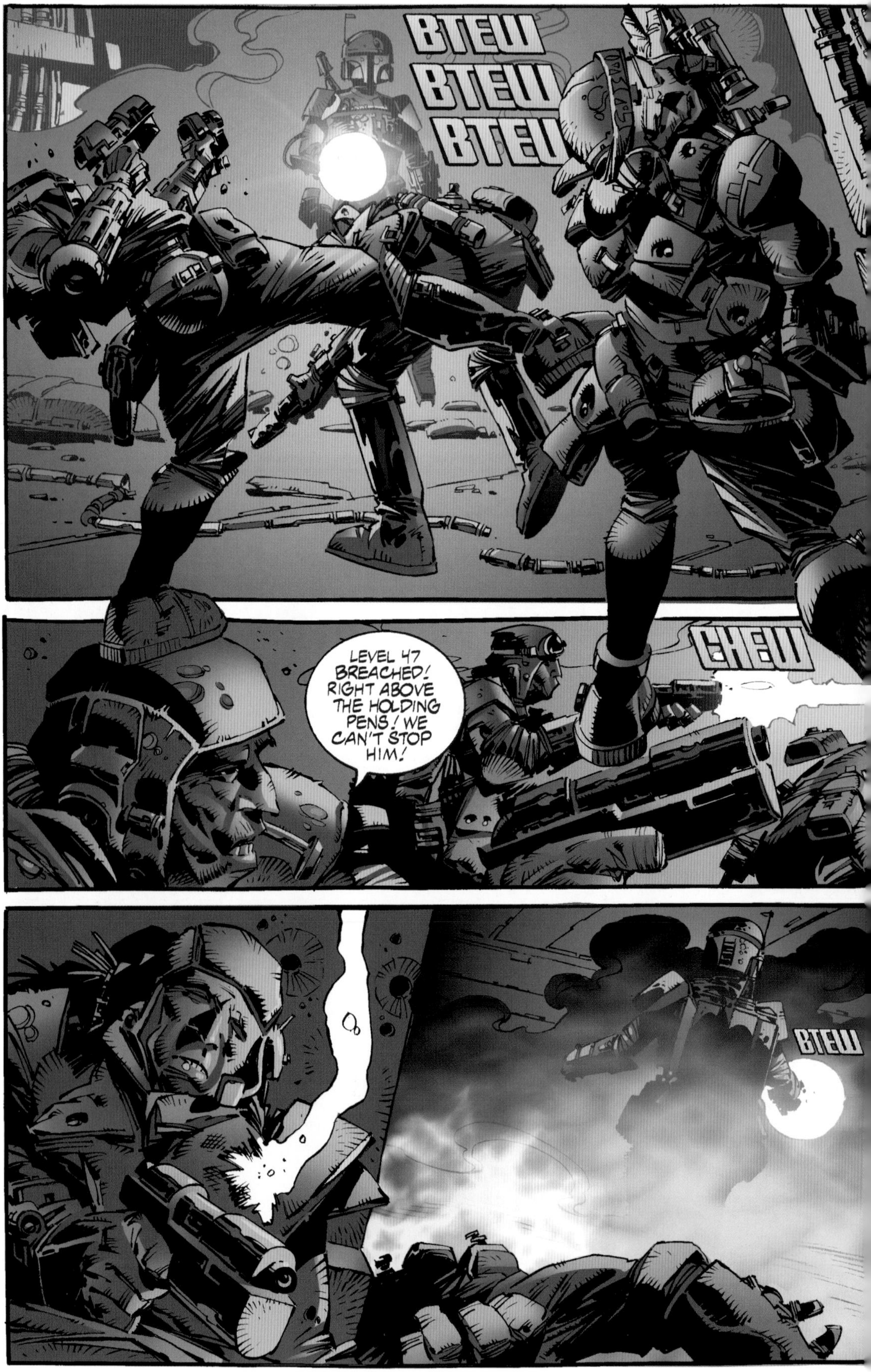
BTEU
BTEU
BTEU
LEVEL 47 BREACHED! RIGHT ABOVE THE HOLDING PENS! WE CAN'T STOP HIM!
CHEW
BTEU

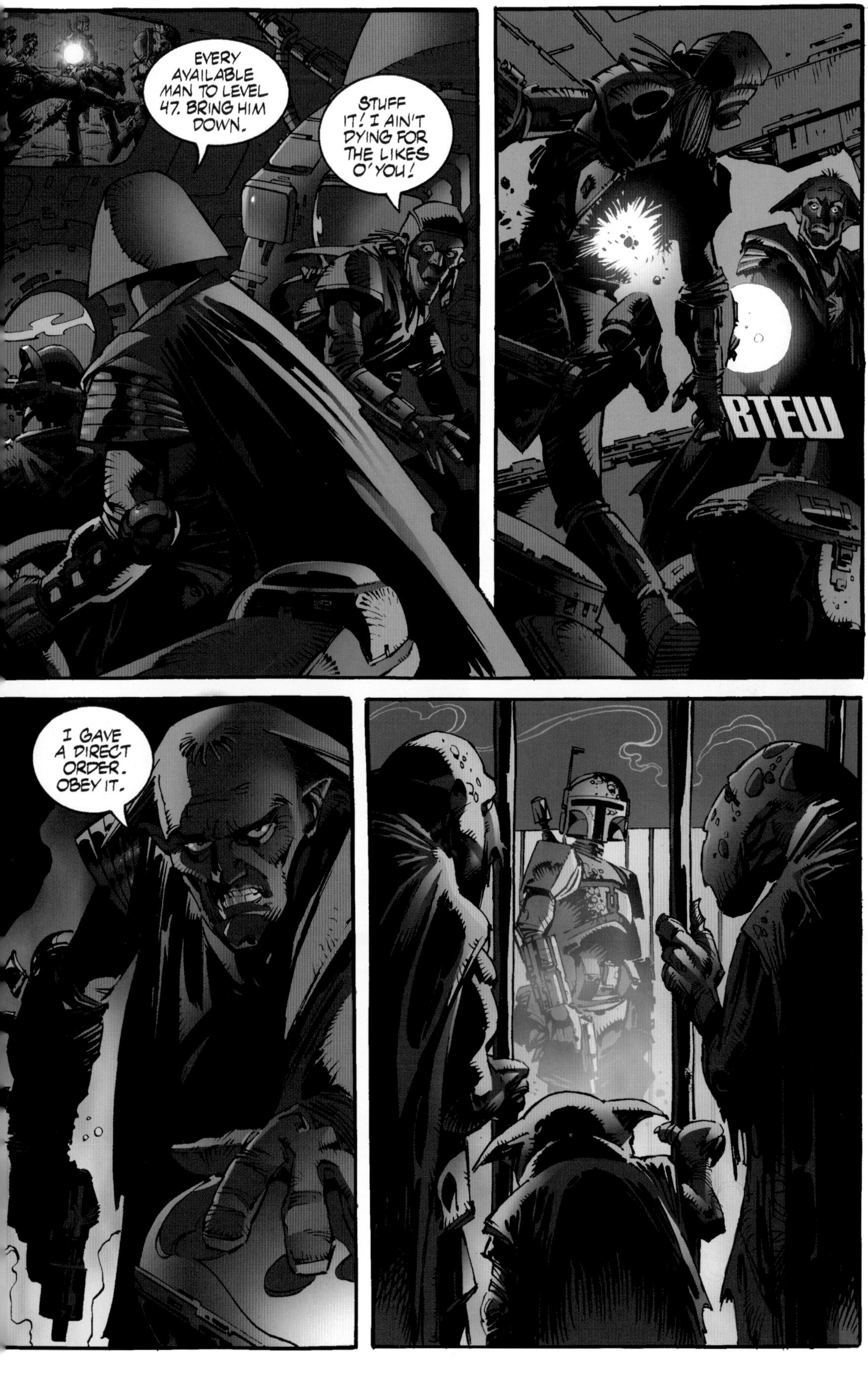
EVERY AVAILABLE MAN TO LEVEL 47. BRING HIM DOWN.
STUFF IT! I AIN'T DYING FOR THE LIKES O' YOU!
BTEW
I GAVE A DIRECT ORDER. OBEY IT.

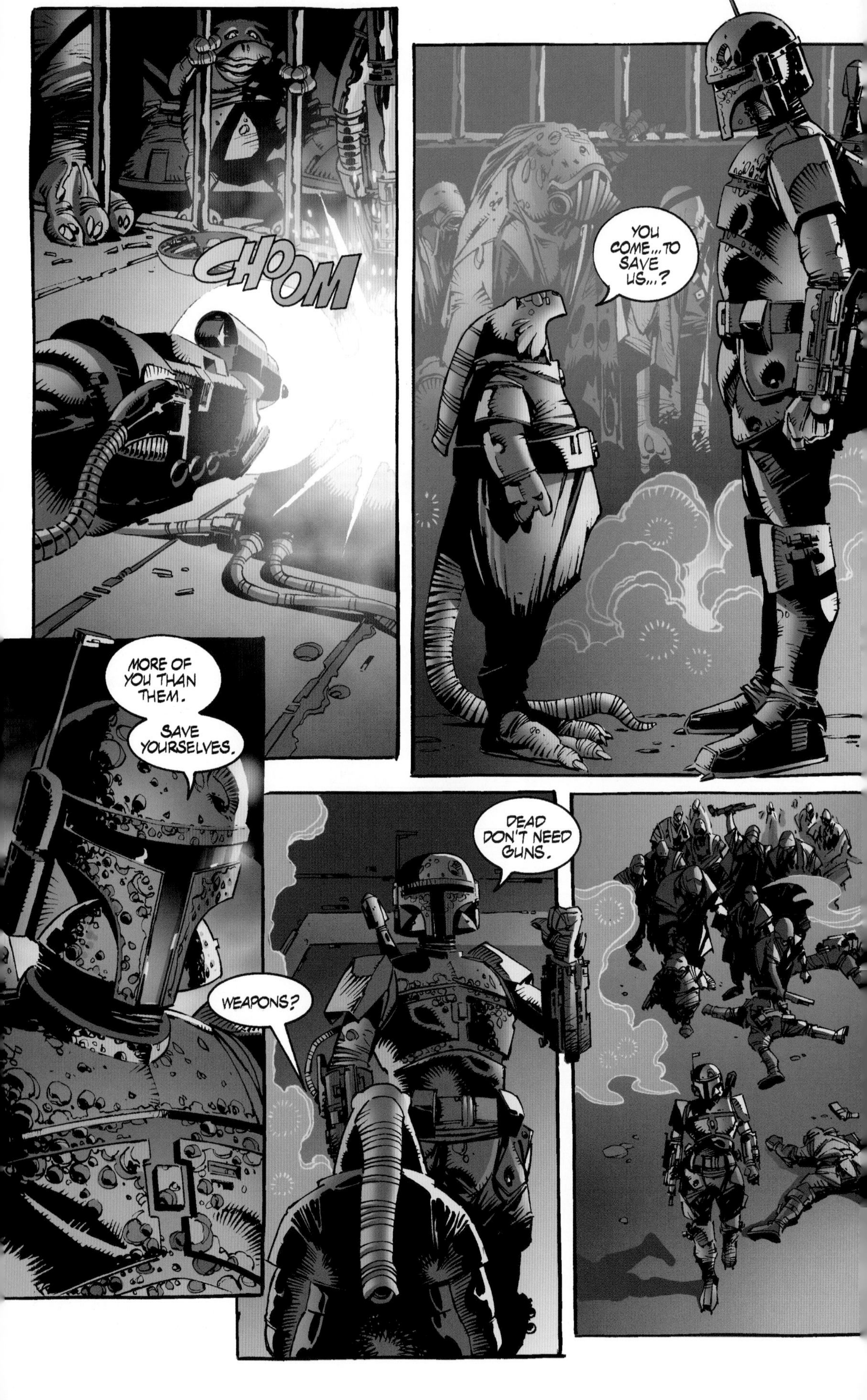
CHOOM
YOU COME... TO SAVE US...?
MORE OF YOU THAN THEM.
SAVE YOURSELVES.
WEAPONS?
DEAD DON'T NEED GUNS.

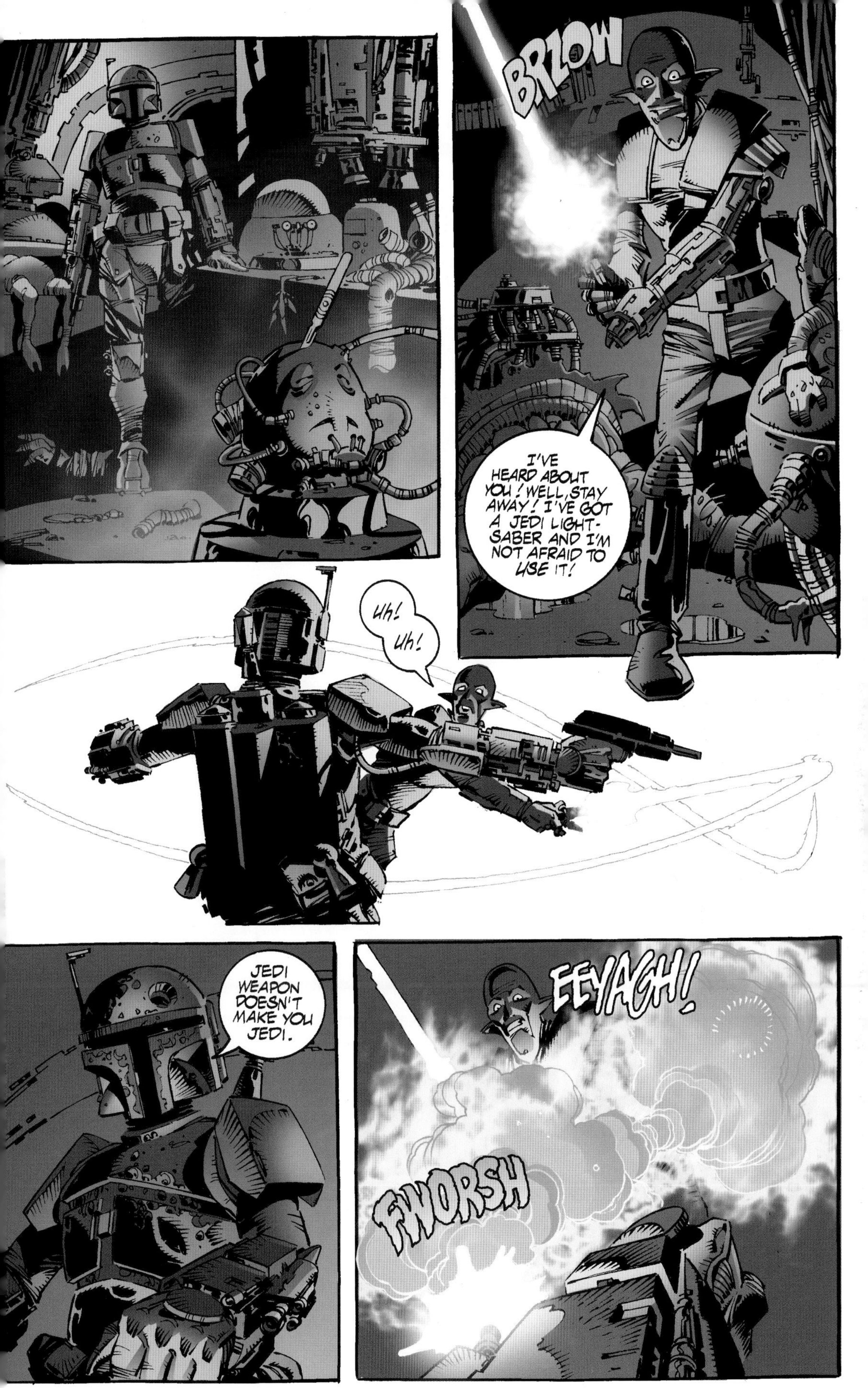
BRZOW
I'VE HEARD ABOUT YOU! WELL, STAY AWAY! I'VE GOT A JEDI LIGHT-SABER AND I'M NOT AFRAID TO USE IT!
uh! uh!
JEDI WEAPON DOESN'T MAKE YOU JEDI.
EEYAGH!
FWORSH

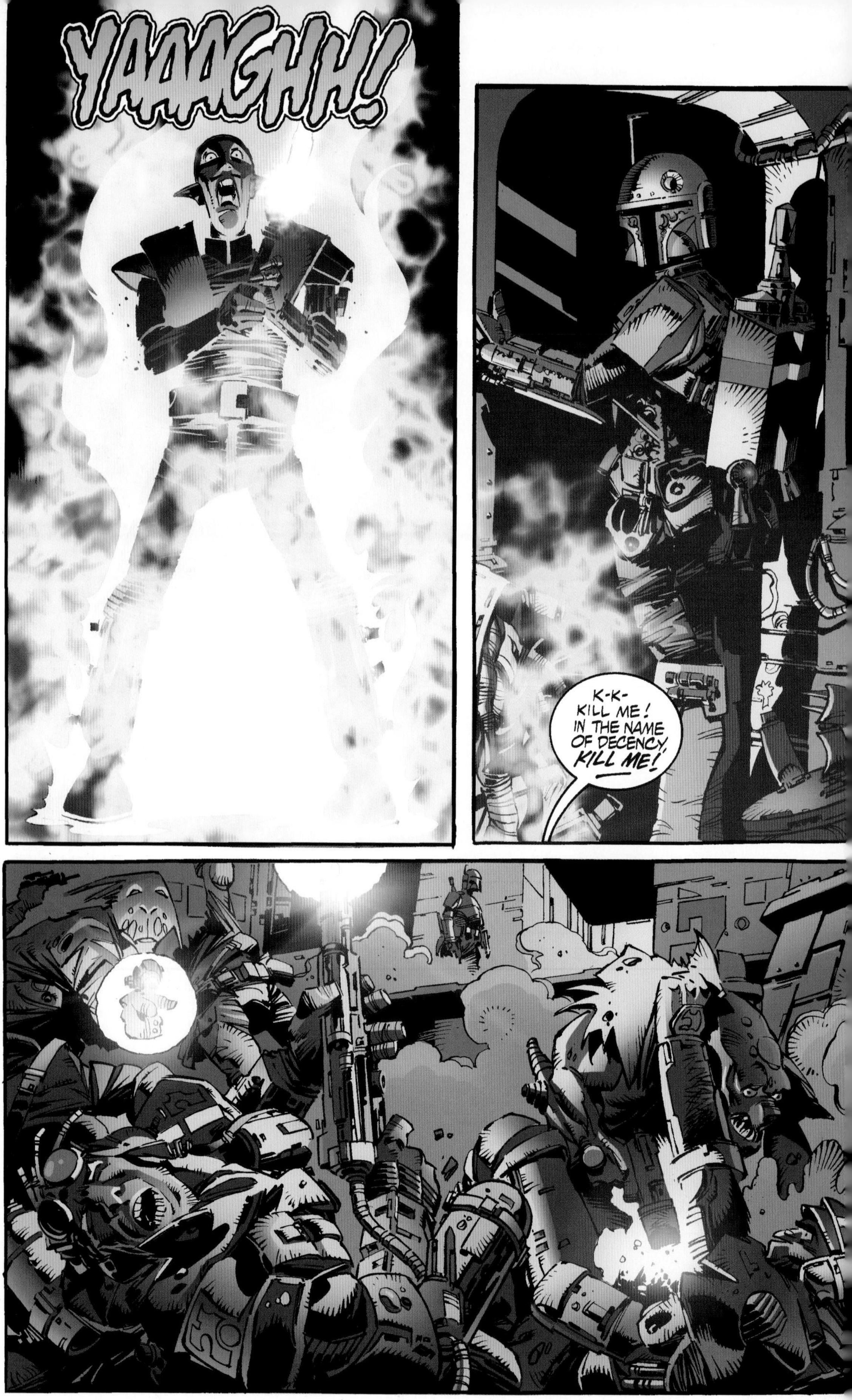
YAAAGHH!
K-K-KILL ME! IN THE NAME OF DECENCY, KILL ME!

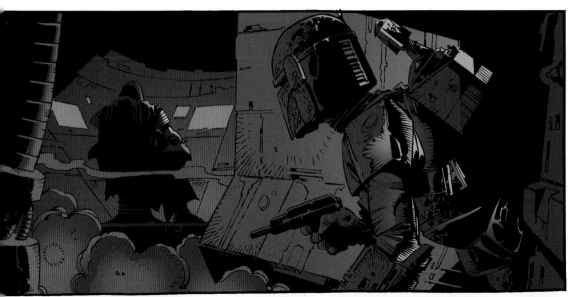

THINK TWICE BEFORE YOU PULL THAT TRIGGER.

THE SELF-DESTRUCT SWITCH IS ACTIVATED. EVEN IN DEATH, I CAN AND WILL DESTROY THIS SHIP AND EVERYONE ON IT. INCLUDING YOU.

LATER.

WHAT DO YOU MEAN?

ESCAPE. HIDE. FIND YOU LATER. KILL YOU THEN.

NO! I'LL NOT SPEND THE REST OF MY LIFE HIDING FROM THE LIKES OF YOU! TURN!

DAMN YOU! I SAID *TURN!*

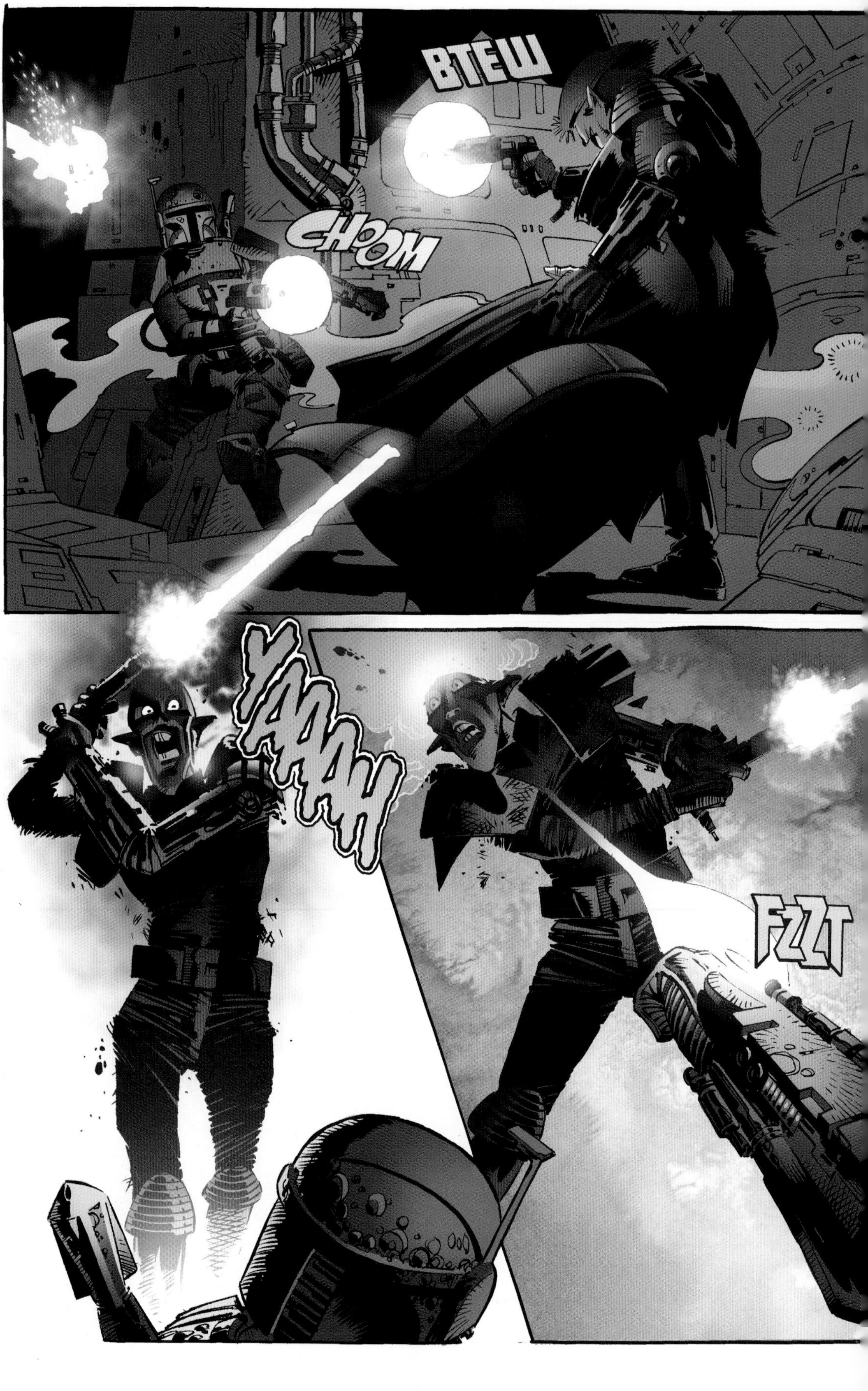
BTEW
CHOOM
YAAAH
FZZT

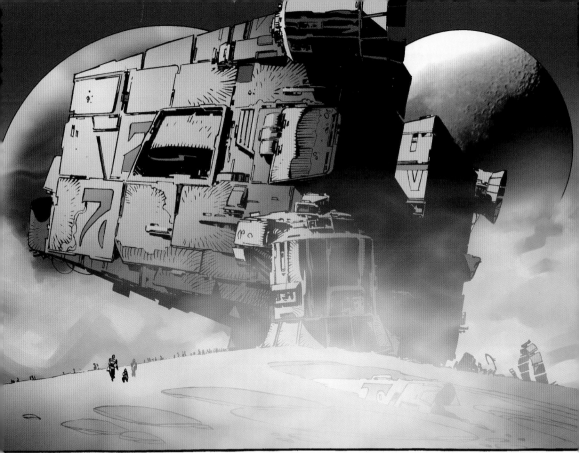

PLEASE... SIR... WHAT DO WE DO *NOW?*

NOT MY CONCERN.

SURVIVE. TAKE THE PLANET. CALL FOR HELP. UP TO YOU.

THE NAME IS BOBA FETT.

REMEMBER THAT.

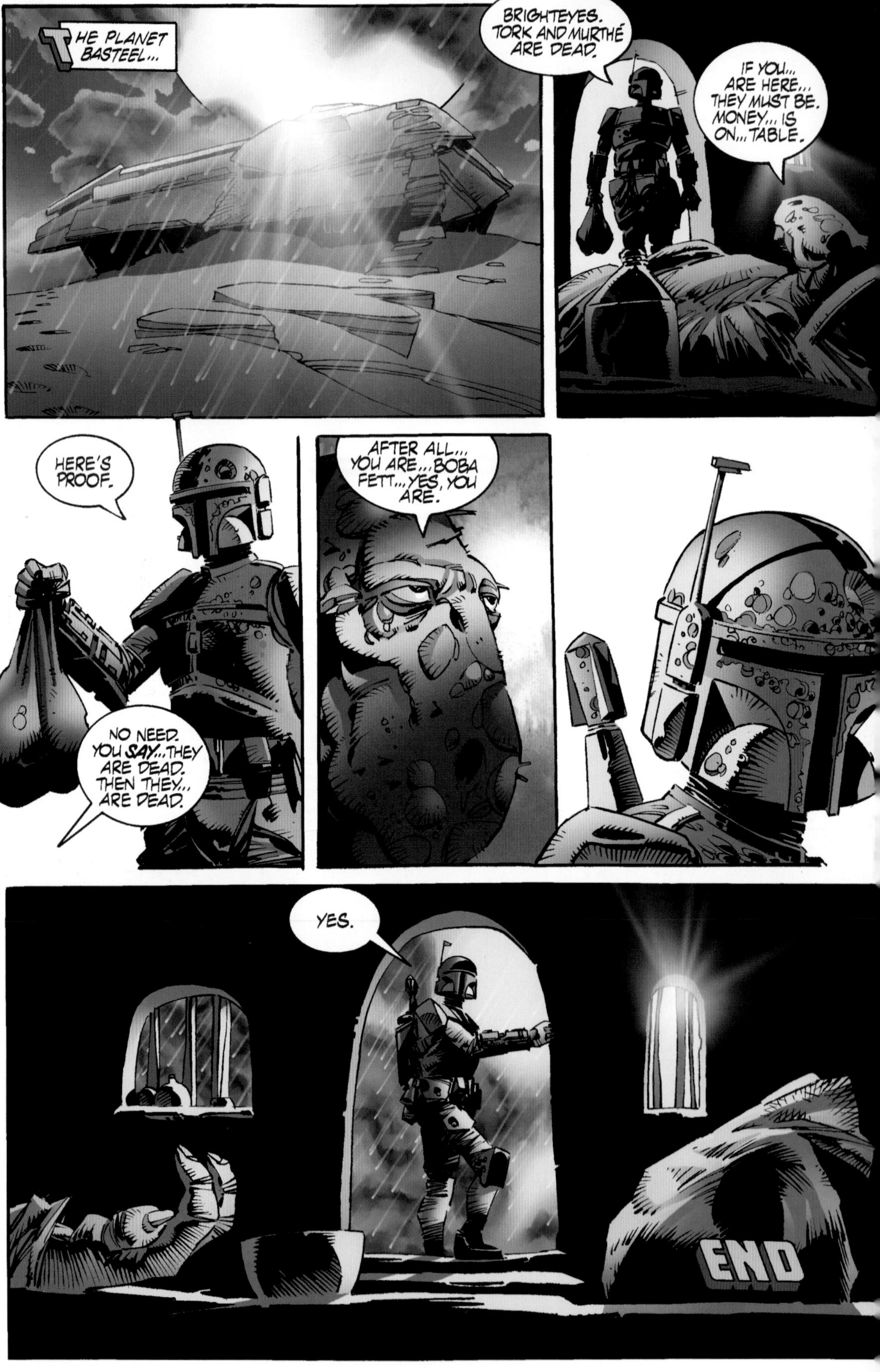
THE PLANET BASTEEL...
BRIGHTEYES. TORK AND MURTHÉ ARE DEAD.
IF YOU... ARE HERE... THEY MUST BE. MONEY... IS ON... TABLE.
HERE'S PROOF.
NO NEED. YOU **SAY**... THEY ARE DEAD. THEN THEY... ARE DEAD.
AFTER ALL... YOU ARE... BOBA FETT... YES, YOU ARE.
YES.
END

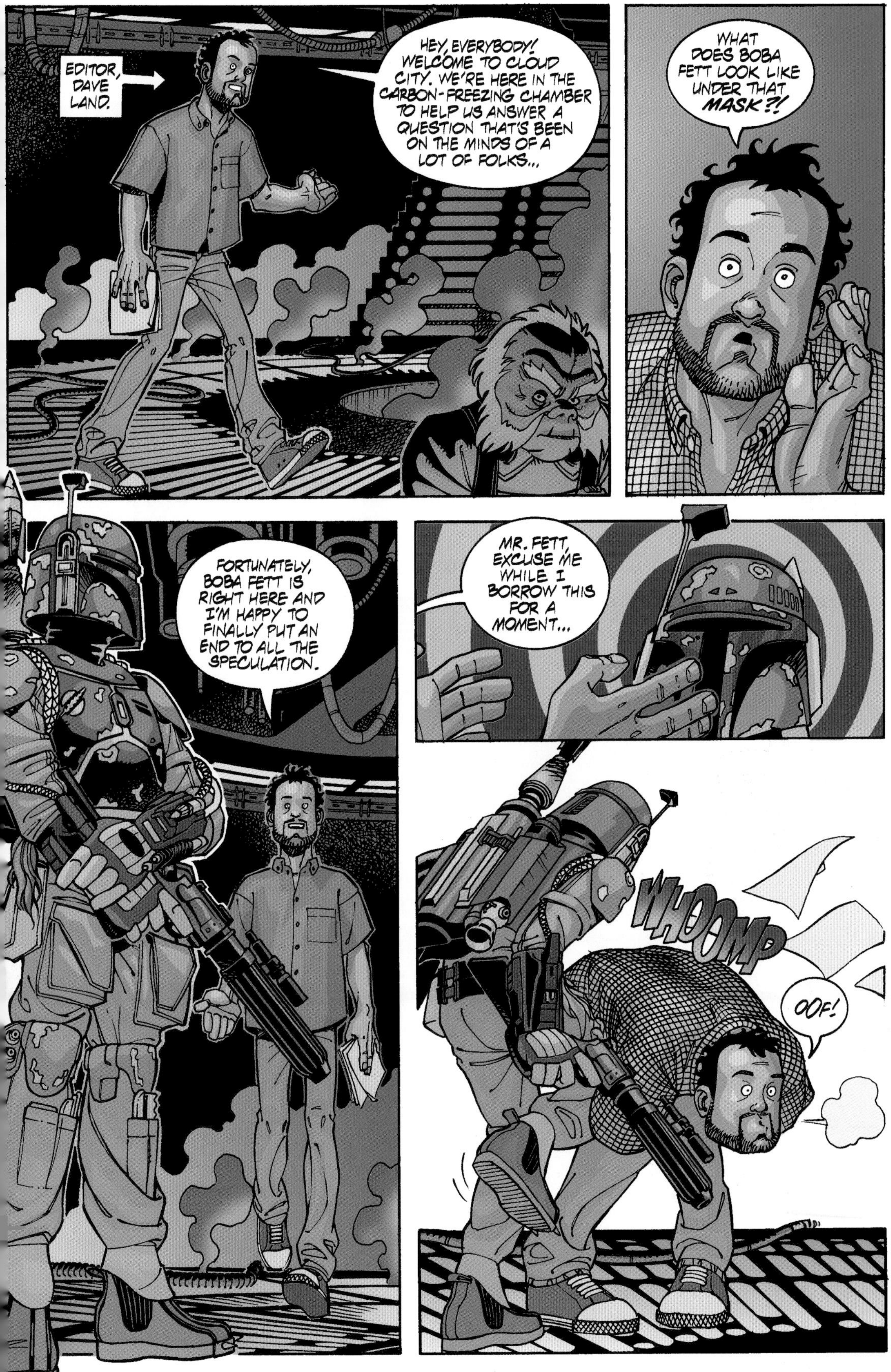
EDITOR, DAVE LAND.
HEY, EVERYBODY! WELCOME TO CLOUD CITY. WE'RE HERE IN THE CARBON-FREEZING CHAMBER TO HELP US ANSWER A QUESTION THAT'S BEEN ON THE MINDS OF A LOT OF FOLKS...
WHAT DOES BOBA FETT LOOK LIKE UNDER THAT MASK?!
FORTUNATELY, BOBA FETT IS RIGHT HERE AND I'M HAPPY TO FINALLY PUT AN END TO ALL THE SPECULATION.
MR. FETT, EXCUSE ME WHILE I BORROW THIS FOR A MOMENT...
WHOOMP
OOF!

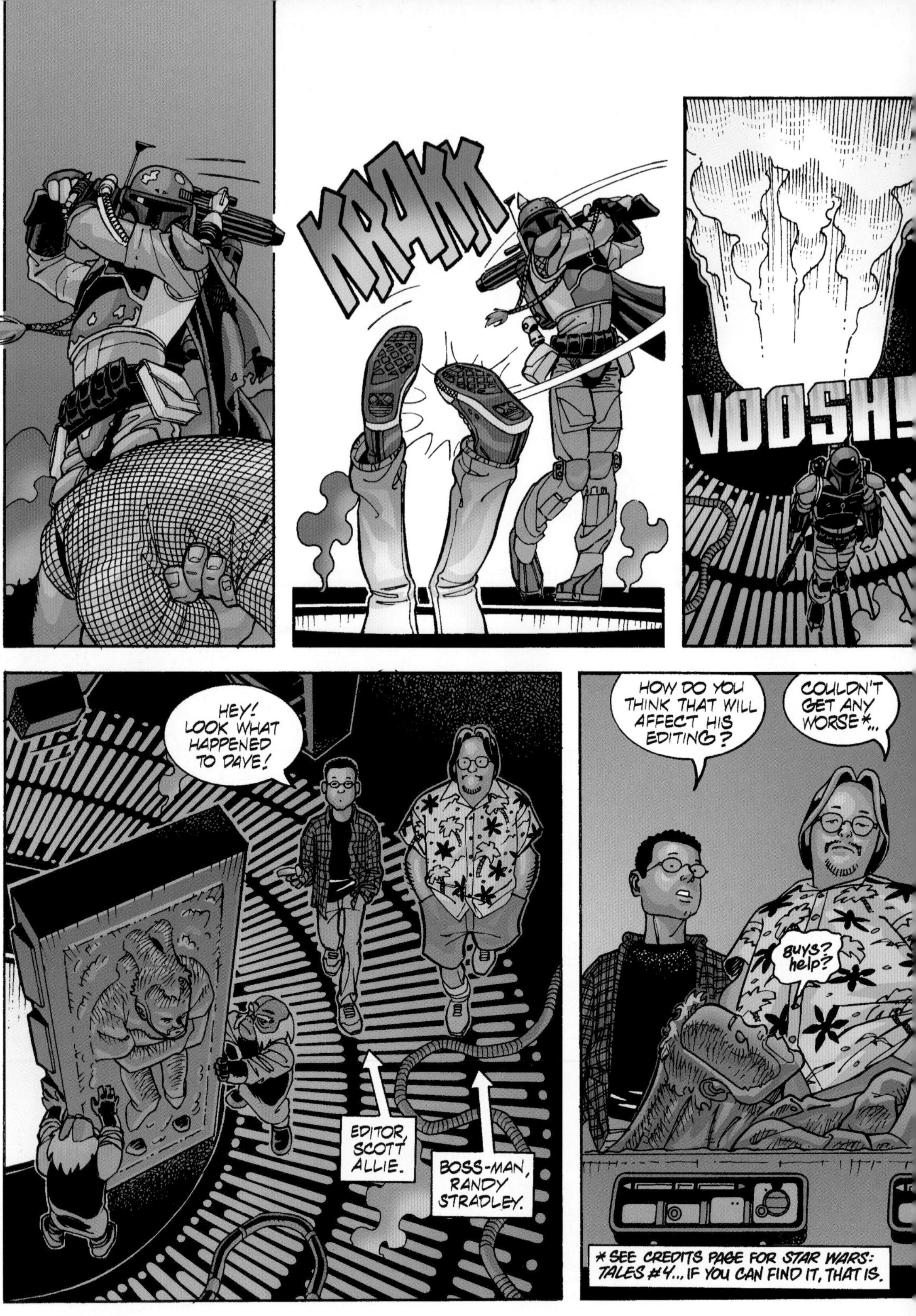
KRAKK
VOOSH!
HEY! LOOK WHAT HAPPENED TO DAVE!
EDITOR, SCOTT ALLIE.
BOSS-MAN, RANDY STRADLEY.
HOW DO YOU THINK THAT WILL AFFECT HIS EDITING?
COULDN'T GET ANY WORSE*...
guys? help?
*SEE CREDITS PAGE FOR STAR WARS: TALES #4... IF YOU CAN FIND IT, THAT IS.

SCRIPT
Dave Land

ART
Lucas Marangon

COLORS
Jason Hvam

LETTERS
Steve Dutro

The fictional character "Randy Stradley" used by permission

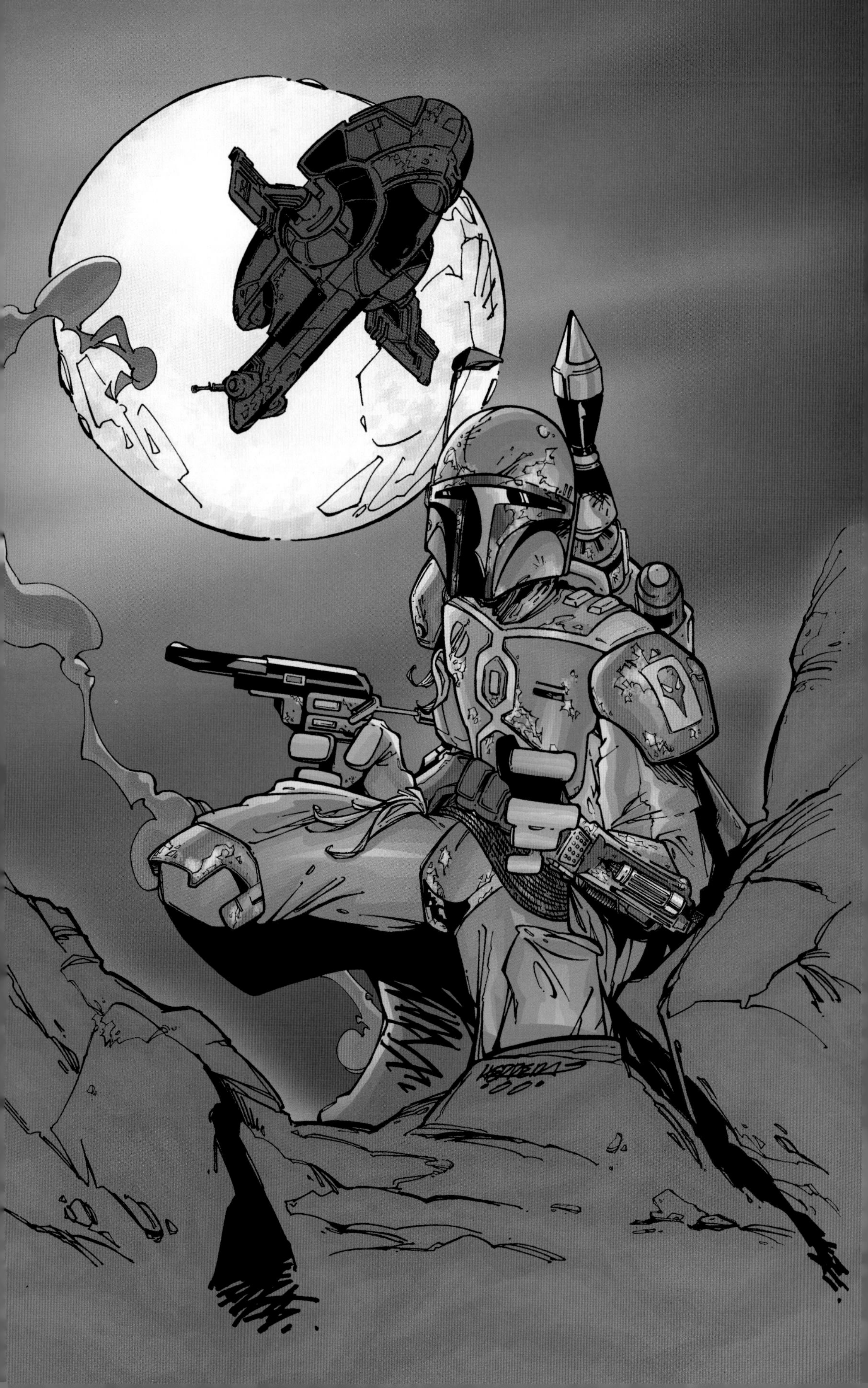

Illustration by Francisco Hererra and Jason Hvam

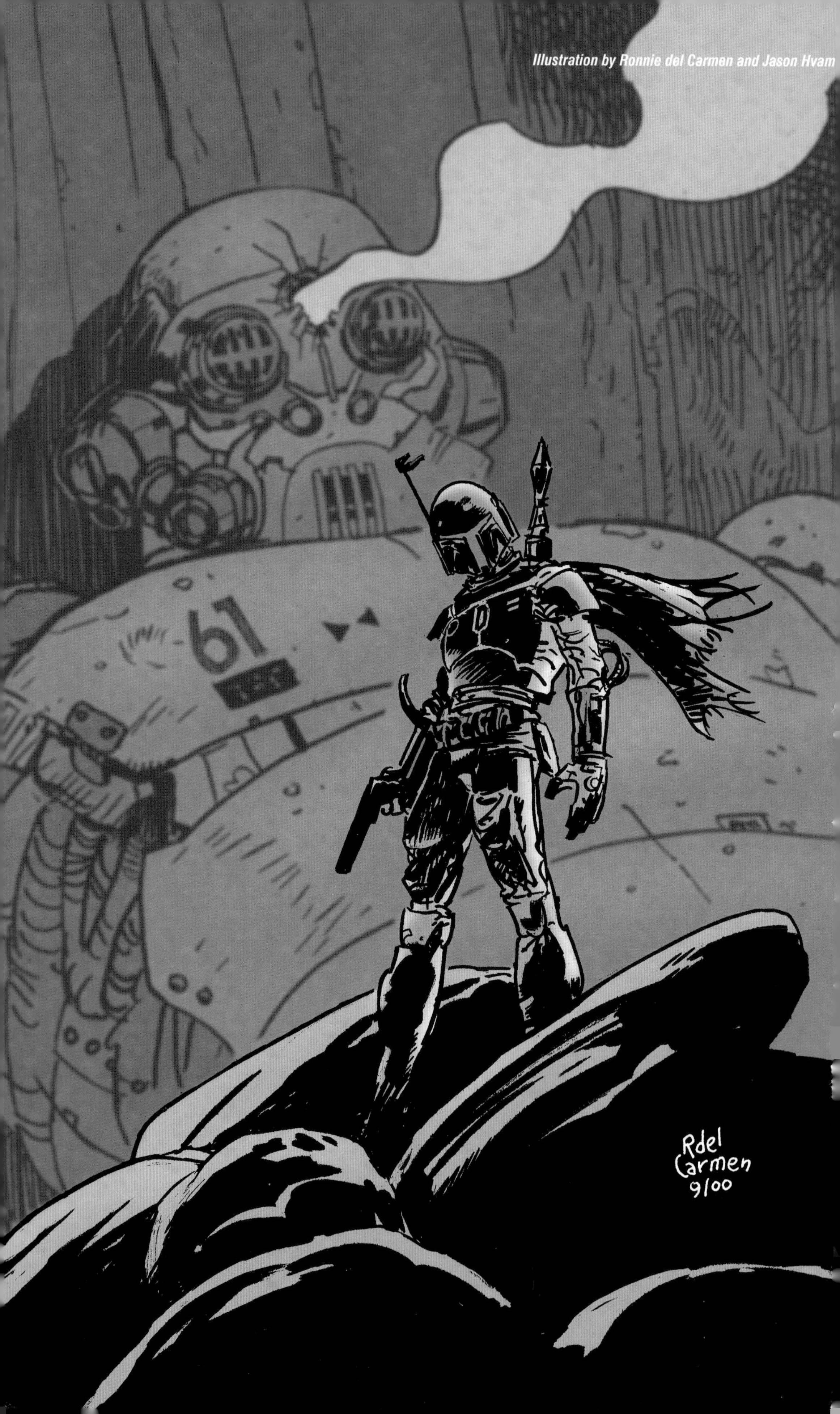
61
Rdel
Carmen
9/00
Illustration by Ronnie del Carmen and Jason Hvam

READY TO TRY SOME OTHER GREAT STAR WARS® TITLES?

STAR WARS
BOBA FETT
ENEMY OF THE EMPIRE
WAGNER GIBSON NADEAU AMASH

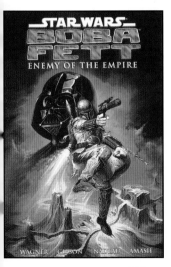

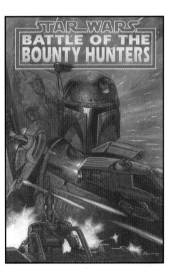

BOBA FETT—ENEMY OF THE EMPIRE

fore the events of *A New Hope*, Darth Vader hires ba Fett to retrieve a single small box, the conts of which could change the fate of the galaxy!

ISBN-10: 1-56971-407-X
ISBN-13: 978-1-56971-407-2
$12.95

STAR WARS
BOBA FETT
Death, Lies, & Treachery

BOBA FETT—DEATH, LIES, AND TREACHERY

Boba Fett pursues a magician who may hold the key to the Hutt's future. The fact that his quarry is dead only poses a slight problem for the bounty hunter . . . not even the dead can escape Boba Fett!

ISBN-10: 1-56971-311-1
ISBN-13: 978-1-56971-311-2
$12.95

STAR WARS
BATTLE OF THE
BOUNTY HUNTERS

BATTLE OF BOUNTY HUNTERS POP-UP BOOK

The first comic book ever fully produced as a pop-up! Boba Fett heads to Tatooine, to deliver Han Solo to Jabba the Hutt. But if Boba thought encasing Solo in carbonite was the hardest part of this mercenary mission, he's in for a surprise!

ISBN-10: 1-56971-129-1
ISBN-13: 978-1-56971-129-3
$17.95

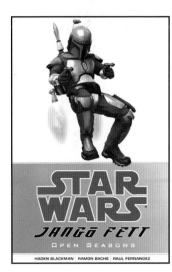

STAR WARS
ZAM WESELL
RON MARZ | TED NAIFEH

ZAM WESELL

go Fett enlists Zam Wesell's help on a mission find and destroy a dangerous artifact. Jango nts to make sure the galaxy is safe for his young son, but Zam's motivations aren't so noble . . .

ISBN-10: 1-56971-624-2
ISBN-13: 978-1-56971-624-3
$5.95

STAR WARS
JANGO FETT

JANGO FETT

When Jango is hired to recover an extremely valuable artifact, he thinks this could be his biggest score. Only one obstacle stands between him and his prize: a beautiful and deadly rival!

ISBN-10: 1-56971-623-4
ISBN-13: 978-1-56971-623-6
$5.95

STAR WARS
JANGO FETT
OPEN SEASONS
HADEN BLACKMAN | RAMON BACHS | RAUL FERNANDEZ

JANGO FETT—OPEN SEASONS

Follow Jango's story from his early farmboy days, through the annihilation of Mandalorian warriors, to his transformation into the galaxy's most feared bounty hunter, and take an in-depth look at the beginning of the infamous Fett legacy.

ISBN-10: 1-56971-671-4
ISBN-13: 978-1-56971-671-7
$12.95

DARK HORSE BOOKS

AVAILABLE AT YOUR LOCAL COMICS SHOP OR BOOKSTORE! • To find a comics shop in your area, call 1-888-266-4226.
For more information or to order direct visit darkhorse.com or call 1-800-862-0052 Mon.-Fri. 9 A.M. to 5 P.M. Pacific Time.
Prices and availability subject to change without notice.

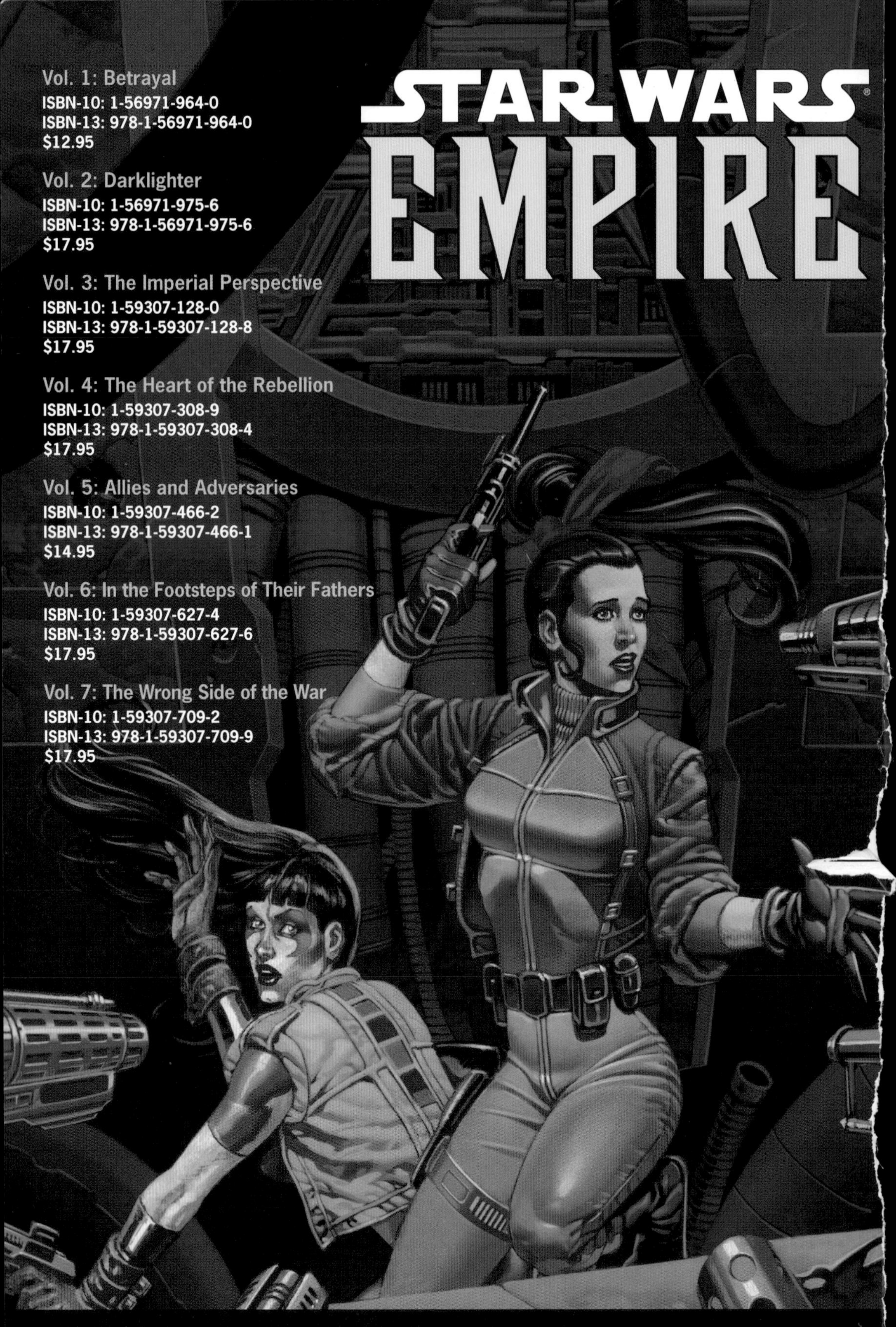

STAR WARS EMPIRE

Vol. 1: Betrayal
ISBN-10: 1-56971-964-0
ISBN-13: 978-1-56971-964-0
$12.95

Vol. 2: Darklighter
ISBN-10: 1-56971-975-6
ISBN-13: 978-1-56971-975-6
$17.95

Vol. 3: The Imperial Perspective
ISBN-10: 1-59307-128-0
ISBN-13: 978-1-59307-128-8
$17.95

Vol. 4: The Heart of the Rebellion
ISBN-10: 1-59307-308-9
ISBN-13: 978-1-59307-308-4
$17.95

Vol. 5: Allies and Adversaries
ISBN-10: 1-59307-466-2
ISBN-13: 978-1-59307-466-1
$14.95

Vol. 6: In the Footsteps of Their Fathers
ISBN-10: 1-59307-627-4
ISBN-13: 978-1-59307-627-6
$17.95

Vol. 7: The Wrong Side of the War
ISBN-10: 1-59307-709-2
ISBN-13: 978-1-59307-709-9
$17.95

DARK HORSE COMICS

TO FIND A COMICS SHOP IN YOUR AREA, CALL 1-888-266-4226.
For more information or to order direct:
*On the web: darkhorse.com
*E-mail: mailorder@darkhorse.com
*Phone: 1-800-862-0052 Mon.-Fri. 9 A.M. to 5 P.M. Pacific Time.